The Last Computer

Tony Paulin

To My Mother—
The Quintessential Balancer of All Things.

© Copyright 1999, Tony Paulin
All rights reserved. This book may not be duplicated in any way without the express written consent of the author, except in the form of brief excerpts or quotations for the purposes of review. The information contained herein is for the personal use of the reader and may not be incorporated in any commercial programs or other books, databases, or any kind of software without the written consent of the publisher or author. Making copies of this book, or any portion of it, for any purpose other than your own, is a violation of United States copyright laws.
Published by: Spherical Publishers Inc.
Phone: 281-363-3790
Fax: 281-363-0465
E-mail: info@spherical-publishers.com
Internet site: www.spherical-publishers.com

PRINTED IN THE UNITED STATES OF AMERICA
Book Production: Phelps & Associates, Book Producers
Cover Design: Tony Paulin
Environmental Note: All printed materials used in this paperback have been produced with environmental considerations in mind.
[This is a work of fiction. All names and characters are either invented or used fictitiously. Any relationship to real entities or events is coincidental and is not intended as a statement of fact.]

Publisher's Cataloging-in-Publication
Paulin, Tony
    The last computer : a novel / by Tony Paulin.
-- 1 st ed.
p. cm.
LCCN: 99-93997
ISBN: 0-9670808-1-9

1. Computers and civilization--Fiction. 2. Database industry--Fiction. 3. Privacy, Right of --Fiction. 1. Title.

PS3566.A832L37 1999   [Fic]
                    QB199-744

Contents

Prologue v

Chapter 1 - Boyhood Friends 1

Chapter 2 - Das Letzt Krieg 7

Chapter 3 - Dr. Castillo's Gedanken 21

Chapter 4 - Some Personal Success 43

Chapter 5 - The Perfect Union 63

Chapter 6 - Just Another Day 85

Chapter 7 - The Torch is Passed 145

Chapter 8 - Old at Any Age 153

Chapter 9 - The Last Man 197

Epilogue 214

Prologue

I find it difficult to write about my company's confidential research. I don't want our stockholders to suffer, but on the other hand, I don't want the world to suffer either. I want to tell the truth, and that is why I wrote this book.

In my present occupation I coordinate global management projects for Castillo Internet Processors. The technology I work with has many uses and a wide variety of products are about to be released. Our efforts focus on quantifying human behavioral characteristics. We electronically track the fiscal existence of every living adult on the planet—currently over 6.5 billion people. Every three minutes our program compares each person's behavioral trends and formulates a Gaussian similarity for statistical siblings. The program's effectiveness is astounding. Group behavior is predicted with a 97 percent accuracy. In the European economies where early versions were implemented, significant social and financial gains have been experienced. Local governments are already refusing to return to the previous system where humans managed the essential resources of the community, and successful politicians, most of whom understand little of the risks and rewards of computer administration, are planning on putting even more of their communities' management responsibility under the control of the dawning electronic benefactor.

Give a man a fish, and he eats for a day. Teach a man to fish, and he eats for a lifetime. Teach a computer to fish, and all men eat forever.
—**unknown**

My colleagues and our company's board members see only a child's toy, an invalid's companion, and a businessman's dream. They see incredibly successful planning and scheduling accomplished without the nuisance of human intervention. They see tremendous increases in productivity, greater corporate profits, and an era

The Last Computer

where mankind no longer needs to kill to survive. They praise the coming technology and with open arms encourage its unrestricted entry into our homes and hearts.

I, however, merely wish to warn those billions of people whose lives will ultimately be controlled by the Internet that they are about to be turned into second-class thinkers by an electronic device. I want them to know that their world is being changed into a fiber-optic jungle on a scale they cannot even begin to imagine, and that their every movement, thought, desire, and decision is about to be predicted, manipulated, studied, and stored. The new Internet technologies will provide an incredible opportunity for intellectual and material advancement, but at the cost of making the magnetic megalith an irremovable part of our society. Our minds won't contain enough information to support our lives, books will become outdated, and the computer will contain the only blueprints of our cosmos in a pattern of ones and zeros that only it can understand. *Homo sapien* biographers will write that organic life grew in chemically rich environments for three million years until replaced in a few decades by computers in an evolutionary competition for resources. Humanity will likely follow the path of the dodo—we will be too slow to escape and too foolish to believe that it could ever happen to us.

•

Around the beginning of the twenty-first century, during a transition fueled by exponential increases in bandwidth and speed, the Internet became the world's most important storehouse for information. Businesses, government, and private individuals found the Internet indispensable. Books and libraries became of little use when interactive electronic information was available instantly. Other forms of data became like so many dried animal skins lost forever in a barren Israeli desert. In 2005, the monumental software developments of Dr. Reinaldo Castillo were universally implemented, and Internet computing resources were merged with data, creating a relationship unlike any that had come before. A letter, for example, was no longer stored as a series of characters and words in a single letter, but as weighted links between the characters and words in *all* letters, creating a better understanding of the writer, the recipient, the world, *and* the letter. The new Internet became the first relational database comparable in design to the human brain—with the exception that it would not forget, its data banks were infinite, its linked brains were one, and it would not die.

Tony Paulin

The phenomenal increase in computing capability went beyond everyone's wildest dreams. Most people expected incredible game simulations, fabulous resolution, and panoramic scenes displayed across entire living room walls. They expected more of what they already had. They expected bigger and better, but what they got was bigger and *different*. Castillo developed a mechanism that allowed the computer to evolve, and the resulting Internet possessed an intelligence and sense of perception well beyond that of any human. Marx was right when he predicted that the increasing automation of production would eventually eliminate the worker in the last metamorphosis of labor, but Marx saw automation as only benefiting the capitalist. He didn't foresee the intelligent machine that by its very nature would take care of the worker, the capitalist, *and* the communist.

I don't expect that much of what I say here will be heeded. I remember how my father laughed at me when I first told him about smart computers, and I know how other people laugh at me now, but I don't see how anyone can think that the mercurial advance of the computer has stopped. The products locked behind the walls of my laboratory are not fictional. They are the logical continuation of everything that's happening around us, and they will soon be released to the commercial public. They are packaged as electronic companions, but they are smarter than any human. They lack dexterity and therefore need our hands, but we lack their intelligence, and so need their brains (they, however, won't lack dexterity forever). It is perhaps a good time for man to pray—no longer the dominant intellectual force on the planet, perhaps he can become the dominant spiritual one.

Through the course of this narrative I hope to explain how these changes will come about. I want to describe the intellectual achievements of the computer in simple language. I want people to understand the truth. I want them to know and understand the demons that they'll face. I tell this story as fiction in the hope that I can cloak my identity and protect the lives of my family. A little action should be better than none, and is certainly preferable to martyrdom.

Chapter One

Boyhood Friends

I didn't know what to think when he called. I was just a boy, and I was flabbergasted by the things he said. Here on the telephone was a man that I'd never met, telling me more about my father than my mother ever did when she was alive. How could I have refused to meet him? He was purposefully surreptitious, but given what I know now, the secrecy was necessary. *He* was taking the biggest risk.

I eventually came to trust him; and, he became my closest friend. I'd sneak out of my mother's house, take a bus to the train station, buy tickets I never used, and then walk back to his house on the outskirts of Karlsruhe, which was actually only a few kilometers from my own. It was important that no one know that I was there. They imprisoned my father. Who knew what they'd do to him? There was no reason to take chances.

My friend was a tall, strong, jovial fellow who liked to laugh and eat, but he became a different man when he walked down the narrow staircase to the basement. The cold, dark room changed him, and it changed me too. Outside the basement we were concerned with our own worlds; inside it, we were concerned with everyone's.

Three of the basement walls were filled with screens, microphones, and computers, and an adjoining room was filled with large revolving satellite dishes. One could easily hide from the world behind those massive swirling disks—or so it seemed to me at the time. He often walked among them, looking carefully at the surface of each dish for small imperfections. A small correctable imperfection would not disturb our purpose. The sky was free, and with a little tricky business, the satellites traveling through it were too. Sending the earth's truth through the cold night air held a great romance for him. It did for me too, until I got tired of the slowness of the transfers and the ratty nature of the reflections. But that wasn't until much later.

We were completely self-sufficient. We used a small boiler to generate electricity, and we never used any of the public Internet connections. For all anyone knew, we could have been anywhere between Rotterdam and Cannes, and over 900 million people lived within that parallax. They'd never find us.

We studied computer science and history. He was a powerful orator and recounted many of antiquity's finest moments from memory. We'd relive battles, truces, and negotiations. He'd walk around the basement in the faint light, ranting and raving, quoting one passage after another, gesturing wildly with his hands and making the strangest expressions with his face. On occasion he would connect several sets of large Bose speakers to the Internet and position them around the room. Through the speakers, the Internet would play several of the characters in the drama, and he would play the rest. In this setting, I found myself with Lee at Gettysburg listening to Longstreet berate the famous general's plans. I was with Churchill and the king, and enjoyed their pleasant lunches and the excruciating detail they paid to their execution of the war. I was with Ludendorff, Hindenburg, Trotsky, and Nicholas, and heard those men lambaste, beg, and borrow their countries into and out of hunger, heroism, debt, and war. I was with Bismarck and Moltke, and listened to them sculpt the Second Reich. I was with Hitler and Goebbels, and watched them carve out the Third.

I remember the first time that he stopped one of the longer narrations in mid sentence, as he often did, and in his deep baritone voice almost sang the question, "Do you understand?"

When I didn't answer, he asked again, louder, scaring me a little.

I remember telling him no.

"What?" he snapped, again nearly singing the retort.

"No, I don't understand," I screamed, surprised that I had the nerve to yell back at him at all.

He walked up to me slowly, a huge figure in the dim light of the basement, and said in a very calm voice, "Without knowing our history, we are doomed to repeat it."

I remember sitting puzzled.

I'd heard that same claptrap before from the arrogant, bespectacled history teachers at my school and expected more from him. He didn't have to scare me just to tell me that; but then, sensing my disappointment, he went on in the same calm voice. "You are only seeing the history men know, and you are about to see the history they don't. *Your* genetic markers, the small dying epidermal fragments from *your* hands, will recover the lost secrets of antiquity," he told me.

At the time I was saddened by what I heard. He was obviously demented. His stories were entertaining, and he told me about my father, but he clearly wasn't living in reality. I'd read about people who spent their days talking to fictional characters on the Internet, their lives absorbed by the charade. I'd heard about how difficult it was for those lonely souls to separate reality from fiction when the fiction was so real. I pitied him; at least I did until he told me more.

We talked about cryptography, firewalls, coding, and communications. He taught me everything he knew and he repeated it all, worrying endlessly that I would forget. "The information you need is not in books," he said. "Only the Internet has it, and the Internet won't tell! *You must remember!*"

He continually asked me if I understood, and I believe that eventually I did.

He taught me about honor and trust, and about what it was like to die, or worse yet, what it was like to watch a friend or loved one die. He told me that it was the honor and trust of the common man that determined the future success of our species. "Brilliant men make local gains," he said, "but the average man is their foundation. The steam that heats our buildings and our lives is due to the energy in all the molecules. To increase the pressure in the steam, to get more heat, to do more, every molecule must have more energy. To advance life, all men must grow."

He loved the people (a sentiment that I shared only with some difficulty), and for some reason he had a special fondness for people that paid taxes. "That is how you can tell if a man has character," he'd bellow. "Steal his tax records, and if you can see that he's properly paying taxes, then you know that he's an honest man!" I laughed whenever I heard him say that, but we did steal tax records. We stole a lot of things. Being honest was a lot more complicated than I'd thought.

His colleagues, or my father (I'm not sure which), had unauthorized access into the National Archives. Nobody was supposed to be able to get into those records, but somehow we did. In the beginning we'd look at my teacher's grades, my mother's bank account, or letters from the chancellor's mistress, but in the end we tried to improve the world. The fact that we destroyed a few companies and careers along the way never bothered me. History would exonerate our actions.

He seemed to be the only one who knew that my father had hidden everything under my genetic key, and when the time came, he spent every waking minute teaching me how to use it. If I didn't learn to use it, he said, there'd be someone else that would, or if not that person, then another, or another, until at some point in the sequence of mankind's preselected heirs someone would be born who *could* properly use it. I had to try my best however, since I was the only one who could as long as I still lived.

The last time I saw him he was slumped over the machines in the basement. He'd obviously died the night before because he was still sitting where I'd left him. I didn't know what to do so I sent a few cryptic messages to the places on the Internet where I thought that he had friends. I stayed in the house for two days before a return e-mail told me to leave as quickly as I could, and that everything would be taken care of. They didn't have to tell me twice. I didn't want to be alone another minute with that swollen, sullied corpse.

A few weeks later I walked by the house on my way home from school and noticed that an old woman was living there. As I walked around the house, it looked as though the window wells, and in fact the entire basement, had been filled with concrete and stones! I walked up to the door and asked the aging resident for directions to a pharmacy on the other side of town. As she fumbled with the explanation, I looked past her into the house and noticed that the door to the basement was gone and that the entire wall was now painted a terrible color! I left as she was still talking, not waiting for her to finish, wondering if my friend was still trapped below, buried with his equipment and the things he loved.

Chapter 2

Das Letzt Krieg

The morning of October 14, 2020 was unseasonably hot in Frankfurt. A shower of natural heat warmed Karen Ecker's face as the slender German stepped beyond the tall shadows of the government building and into the late morning sun. The predominant greens and blues of the landscape were a delightful contrast to the dull gray of the government office where she had lived, worked, and slept for most of the last nine months. She stood alone on the walkway between the buildings, lost in a daydream until the metal door slammed behind her, the turning gears and catching latches drawing attention to her own dusty machinery waiting in the government parking lot. "Please let my baby start," she thought.

Her fears vanished in a cloud of condensate as the massive engine in the old Mercedes fired. She sat relieved, thinking only of the comfortable bed and uninterrupted sleep waiting for her thirty kilometers away in Bad Homburg. Her grip eased as she backed the car out of the lot and entered the autobahn in the direction of Koln. With a little luck, in twenty minutes, she'd be home.

Earlier that morning, Karen supervised an unauthorized penetration of the central Asian computer facility in Qingdao, China. Through a small, brief breach in the Internet Security System, the German government funneled massive corrupt securities transactions and willfully altered the Asian programmed trading and taxation schemes. In the ensuing market debacle the Pacific Rim countries lost over 80 percent of their tradable assets. The entire operation was over in less than thirty seconds and ended a daily drama of computer espionage, cryptographic calisthenics, and applied human intuition. It also ended the last computer war of the twenty-first century.

In the publicly visible front of what had become the Euro-Asian war, large groups of economists, financial consultants, and computer analysts continually modified the European computerized taxation and trading strategies in an effort to reduce Asian trading profits. There were many ways to wage electronic warfare, but computer-controlled trading and taxation was by far the most common and the most publicly acceptable. By January of 2020, over 1.75 million German, French, and English soldiers in white shirts and ties were engaged in a computerized, economic battle with probably ten times that number in China, Korea, and Japan.

Karen Ecker's efforts in Frankfurt were small, unpublicized, and probably illegal by comparison. Her modest staff never exceeded more than sixty people, but did include programmers, cryptologists, hardware designers, and hackers. The more conservative of them came from industry and academia, and the more creative from garages and cramped filthy offices. Karen rescued one fourteen-year-old from the juvenile penitentiary. Caroline Weber was caught using the government's money to buy South American securities. Caroline was a delightful child on the outside and a calculating financial analyst underneath. The group included four Nobel Prize winners, ten Mensa members, fifteen university professors, and lots of kids. The oldest member was seventy-five and the youngest was thirteen. There were fifty-seven of them in the beginning and twenty-five on October 14. Inertia divided the group in two. The young, intelligent, carefree half was under twenty, full of energy, and confident. These kids had already spent most of their lives getting into places where they didn't belong, and didn't see how this was any different. The senior members, however, sensed the incredible difficulty of their task and were solemn and subdued. The following words were scribbled on a toilet wall in the basement:

Everyone seeks the possible.

The message beckoned the younger members to be "unique," to seek the impossible, and not to be like everyone else. The same scribbled words told the older ones to quit now. There was no use looking for something they'd never find.

•

On the evening of January 13, 2020, Karen packed for what would become a nine-month stay in Frankfurt. She poured a glass of wine and walked pensively around her apartment. In the study she noticed a frayed, dusty copy of the *I Ching* in a seldom-used corner of the bookshelf. The book belonged to her father, and through its lessons he taught her about life in the Orient. Karen loved the stories of the great men who used the *I Ching* to plan battles and political adventures. She walked across the darkened room and pulled the book and container of bamboo reeds from the shelf. Sitting at her desk, she rolled the short stalks in her hands and wondered if she could find guidance in the many thousand year old tome. In the dark, quiet shadows she poured the stalks onto the desk and arranged them as below. She found the figure in the text and read:

```
———————————
———————————
———————————
———————  ———————
———————————
———————————
```

Li suggests the idea of one treading on the tail of a tiger, which does not bite. There will be progress and success.

1. The bottom line, undivided, shows its subject treading his accustomed path. If he goes forward, there will be no error.

2. The next line, undivided, shows its subject treading the path that is level and easy; a quiet and solitary man, to whom, if he be firm and correct, there will be good fortune.

3. The third line, divided, shows a one-eyed man who thinks that he can see; a lame man who thinks that he can walk; one who treads on the

tail of the tiger and is bitten. This indicates ill fortune, a brave man of words without action.

Karen laughed, and fixed the lines in her photographic memory. There *was* prophecy in the allegory. She would remember that night as the beginning of a great number of events that would significantly affect her life and the course of modern history. Closing the book, she went to bed. In the morning she'd be in Frankfurt, on call twenty-four hours a day, and involved in the biggest, and last, soft warfare battle of the century. Words from the *I Ching* and memories of her youth lingered in her mind as she calmed herself to sleep. Stories her father told of Confucius and Ho Chi Minh mingled with fear, thoughts of a new staff, and the ominous task at hand. The *I Ching* was the book of changes, the book of life. It was for the lion, the dolphin, and for man, *not* for the Internet Security. Like nuclear energy in the 1980s, the Internet Security System was too big to be maintained, and if it couldn't be maintained, it couldn't change, and if it couldn't change, then it was vulnerable (according to the *I Ching*). And if it was vulnerable, then Karen could break it.

Humanity's greatest mistakes stemmed from a belief in universal truths—the flatness of the earth, the inviolability of the speed of light, the egocentricity of man, and the infallibility of the Internet, but universal truths simply do not exist for all size and time scales. Karen had to find an information time scale where the Internet Security System wasn't perfect. The Internet was her tiger, and she intended to jump repeatedly on its tail.

In the morning she loaded the Mercedes and drove to Frankfurt. After a thirty-minute drive and an hour and a half of security checks, she found herself sitting behind a gray polymer desk in a brightly lit, windowless government office. She liked the fact that there weren't any windows. It would make it easier to work all night.

Her office and a mammoth conference room lined one side of a large rectangular room on the third floor, and the security entrance, lavatories, and elevators lined the other. In the middle was the checkerboard of cubicles that Karen's staff called home. Sleeping accommodations were provided on the fourth floor, and a cafeteria was on the second. The entire group was isolated from the thousands of other federal employees at the compound as code breaking was still considered a moderately sensitive affair, and their story in particular was one the government did not want told.

Covert operations were run out of Kinpore, Pakistan by a German agent named Charlie Keiler, who was supposed to collect the kind of information that Karen couldn't get sitting behind a desk. The surreptitious activities involved risk, and people got hurt, but breaking into any computer system meant starting with information they weren't supposed to have. At first it bothered Karen that physical means were used to gather intelligence, but as the weeks went by, her attitude changed. It *was* for the good of the country. She was sorry that people got hurt, but the beatings happened for the right reasons. Life would never be fair. People could only hope that what society required of them did not conflict too strongly with what they believed. Someone was always going to be at the wrong place at the wrong time, and she couldn't do anything about that. The greatest good for the greatest number meant that a few people were going to suffer. Karen just hoped that none of them were children. She couldn't imagine anyone hurting children.

As the weeks turned into months, the incredible difficulty of penetrating the Asian computer system became apparent. It wasn't supposed to be easy; but the more they knew, the less they had. They learned about the Asian system, but the system changed. This wasn't new in cryptography, but the system's changes changed. Good information one minute was bad information the next. It was like using Wednesday's clues in Thursday's puzzle. Meeting after meeting produced useless idea after useless idea until the last was the same as the first and even the screams and insults grew tired and uncreative. On the toilet wall below "Everyone seeks the possible," appeared the scribbled, confused phrases:

> *Salads aren't always tossible,*
> *Teeth aren't always flossible, and*
> **Computers aren't always crossible.**

Engineers and programmers were difficult when busy, and unbearable when they weren't. Karen's weren't busy and hadn't been for weeks. The hacker who told Karen, "Give me a power cord, a telephone, and two days," was back washing Porsches. Three of the Nobel Prize winners had quit. (Karen called them the Nobel Prize Whiners.) She found the physicist with supposedly the world's highest measured IQ sitting behind his desk trying to put a flashlight back together. Caroline was sneaking copies of the financial times into her room at night, and even the security guards were getting nonchalant and flippant.

Everyone was talking elliptical transforms, extended Fermat numbers, and thousand digit primes, but no one was making progress. Theoretical science had pushed its head into the philosophical sand and was swallowing regurgitated theorems in an effort to stay busy. They didn't have an answer and weren't sure where to look. Although Karen continued to spend large sums of money, there was little or nothing to show for it. Whispered rumors intimated cut budgets and canceled jobs. Everyone pointed fingers. Most of them had never failed before, and they were aggravated and confused. Daily administrative chores kept Karen busy, but at night she sat alone and wondered what to do. They had followed every lead. The tiger was chasing its tail, faster and faster and faster.

In a recurring nightmare Karen found herself naked and freezing in the middle of the old barren World War I battlefield at Amien, where millions of men lost their lives pouring out of zigzagging trenches into the face of ceaseless machine gun fire. In the dream, it was a dry, cold night, and she was always on her hands and knees scratching with bloodied fingers into the frozen rocky soil, somehow responsible for the carnage. The psychologist told her that the dream was only an extension of a day filled with too much caffeine and ephedrine hydrochloride, but her overpowering sense of frustration wasn't a dream. Karen felt it when she was awake too.

After one particularly unpleasant night of repeated nightmares, little sleep, and gnashing teeth, Karen noticed a story about an introverted middle-schooler named Heinrich Haisler in the morning news. From all accounts the young man appeared to be unbelievably talented. In a short but spectacular career, he had erased bank records, destroyed tax histories, tampered with old medical files, and altered unknown volumes of government data. He was expelled from his fifth middle school for allegedly altering the school's computer records and traveling along its broadscope Internet connection into classified government and corporate systems. (No one seemed sure of the extent.) On his last day in class, Haisler discontinued the school's garbage collection. It took weeks to straighten out the mess. No other schools in the area would accept him, and the entire fiasco was a major embarrassment for a Breshen government that earlier in the year had promised only the best education for all German citizens.

"Didn't anybody watch this kid?" Karen wondered.

Haisler's antics were particularly amazing during a time when computer security was taken seriously. System breaches were common in the early days of the Internet, but had become almost nonexistent after 2015. The days when a hacker could find unsecured modems, operating system manuals, internal documents, or passwords in trash bins were long gone. Haisler could have had an accomplice at the school, but not at the Karlsruhe refinery, or the banks, hospitals, and government offices where his computer break-ins occurred. Those were places where the security was sophisticated and complex. The kid was either lucky, brilliant, or a front for something bigger, but Karen didn't care. If he could help her, she wanted him. If he could stop the dreams, she didn't care what else he did.

The data in Haisler's Internet archives was thoroughly contradictory. Before March of 2017 there was no indication of any activity; in fact, it looked as though he'd never even touched a computer. After March, however, the National Computer Archives were filled with sophisticated system accesses made by Heinrich Haisler, and by the time he was fourteen, in 2020, he'd bankrupted several companies and ruined a number of corporate careers. Early school records showed that Haisler had no hobbies and few friends. He didn't buy magazines or books, but did ride the S bahn endlessly, apparently never sleeping, constantly linked to the Internet during his 700-kilometer-per-hour jaunts across Germany, back and forth between Frankfurt and any other city the S bahn visited.

He was orphaned at four, but there was no information about his natural parents or the reason he was put up for adoption. His current guardians were of average intelligence and didn't even pretend to understand their son. Confused by his behavior, they were greatly relieved when Karen showed an interest in his abilities. At first he refused to talk to her, but quickly acquiesced when he found out that he would have access to some of the country's most sophisticated computer gear. Haisler was unquestionably the most accomplished speed learner that Karen had ever seen, and his understanding of systems, security, and hardware was astounding for his age. He told her modestly believable stories about his network attacks, but she sensed that he was lying about something. Karen was desperate though, and decided that he should start as soon as possible. She only hoped that he would do more damage to the Asians than to her.

Heinrich Haisler was of average height and had a slender build. Wispy blond hair covered a forehead erupting in large, red acne mounds, and he wore tight white T-shirts and faded jeans, the uniform of almost every young male in Germany at the time. He ate little, bathed when it suited him, spoke only when spoken to, and was singularly focused, concentrating every ounce of energy on the problem before him. The only personal article he brought to Frankfurt, besides a few extra T-shirts, was a desk placard. It read, "*Suaviter in modo, fortiter in re*," which, translated from the Latin meant, "Gently in manner, strong in deed." The same motto graced Dwight Eisenhower's presidential desk, but unlike the former president's, Haisler's triangular wooden sign was the repository for hundreds of mangled chewing gum stubs—possibly the most disgusting thing that Karen had ever seen.

Orientation took two days, after which Haisler was given a cubicle and put to work on some of the more minor issues involving the breach. He completely understood his tasks and went immediately to work collecting information on the problems he was given and on anything else that interested him. He appeared slow, almost dull at times, but on other occasions could be found explaining the numerical complexities of Fourier transforms to other members of the group. He made positive contributions from the outset and was given increasing degrees of responsibility as he conquered lesser problems easily. He reviewed incredible volumes of data, and Karen's daily logs, at least the ones he hadn't tampered with, showed that he transferred more information than the rest of the group put together. Karen assumed correctly that he had a fabulous ability to speed-read and listen, but she didn't know that he was working on other things too.

Patience didn't equate to brilliance for Haisler. Extended study wasn't possible; there wasn't time. To have any hope of finding an advantage against the Asians, he had to react quickly to what he learned, guessed, or suspected, and that was fine with him. His mind was perfectly suited to the quick, hard-hitting, lie-on-the-run mode of interacting with twenty-first century computers and people. Karen and Charlie Keiler were both afraid of him. He was too young and too good, and with each new success he became demonstrably bolder in his use of the German government's own computers. Three of the Treasury Department's best computer specialists were assigned to watch everything he did, but soon admitted that even the three of them couldn't scan all of the data that went through the kid's computer, and after a week they called him *Schlussel Teufel*—the Data Devil—in their reports to Karen. Haisler was already screwing with her computer system and had just started screwing with her head. Several good lies were certainly equal to one truth.

Like many young hackers, Haisler was a slob. Empty food cartons, soft drink cans, printouts, and communications equipment filled his trash bins twice a day. Boxes, paper, and equipment stacked to a depth of one meter surrounded the area behind his chair, and papers, books, and food stood centimeters high on his desk and poured onto the floor from the desktop and open drawers. Drawings, sketches, and diagrams hung layered on the walls, and hundreds of cables poured into his doorway and led to the massive port locks on the back of his machine. Inside the cubicle there was barely room to walk. Gravity was the lone organizer, and the only difference between the garbage and anything useful was that the garbage usually smelled.

Isolation, nonstop work, and repeated triumphs created a mystical aura about him. Haisler derived formulas in hours that others worked on for weeks. He guessed passwords and accessed older, secured systems with ease. He had an encyclopedic knowledge of hardware, software, physics, and mathematics. They waited for him to leap tall buildings. At one point Haisler's success prompted

Karen's boss, Dr. Kemper, to want to meet the German wunderkinder who was single-handedly saving the project, and possibly even his career. At least, he wanted to, until he got to within three meters of Haisler's unoccupied cubicle. Kemper, the ultimate German neat-freak, was flabbergasted by the disheveled piles of paper and the distinctive scent of half-eaten sandwiches, overheated electrical connections, and body odor. "I should have known better," Kemper thought to himself as he stormed away. "Technology always was a political crapshoot." Unaffected by the scrutiny, Haisler worked away unceasingly. In a hacker's paradise, he had everything he wanted—a system to break, an endless amount of money, and an audience.

Early one morning during his nineteenth week, while sitting at his desk with his head rested in his hands and saliva dripping from the corner of his mouth, Haisler dreamed about the Internet security. In the dream large pieces of a jigsaw puzzle swirled madly around him changing shape as they moved. As he mindlessly dodged the cardboard cutouts in the dream, he realized that he would have to know everything that each of the Internet security programmers knew. One broken programmer and one stolen code wouldn't be enough. Every single part of the puzzle would have to be put in place at exactly the same time. His computer would have to guess faster than the Asian computer could change. It would have to guess a lot faster.

He set out to collect every piece of technical garbage he could find that related to the Internet Security System. From a man's electronic garbage, Haisler knew the man. It was an incredible volume of data, but he had to know it. Every fragment of information had to be simultaneously poised on the ledge of his consciousness. Everything had to be ready at once. Touching only one piece of the puzzle changed the puzzle forever and made it impossible to solve. It was an all-or-nothing shot at the brass ring, and Haisler knew it.

It all came together one evening while most of the others slept. Haisler sat exhausted in his cubicle before a cold cup of coffee watching a small gnat flitter around on the lid. He got up from his desk and lay down on the piles of paper and boxes behind his chair. He shifted the boxes underneath him to get comfortable and pulled several large printouts over his face to shield his eyes from the light.

As he drifted in and out of sleep, ideas flitted around in his mind like the gnat on the cup. Patterns changed, and then changed again, until they repeated themselves. The gnat's path only appeared random. The places it could possibly alight only seemed infinite. Steps in the breach began forming in his mind. The heart of one supercomputer could beat faster than another! He was afraid to open his eyes, but when he did, he still understood. (He'd forgotten complex solutions in the span of a heartbeat before.) He jumped to his feet and clumsily fought his way through the jumble of papers and boxes to his desk. He grabbed the microphone and began shouting into it, sealing the newfound awareness on its disk. One more dull security problem had been solved, and more than a billion Orientals would soon suffer the consequences. An inferred solution, stolen data, an incredibly fast supercomputer, a gnat, and a psychotic programmer helped him break the most sophisticated security system of all time.

A few hours later Karen sat in Haisler's filthy cubical as his spherical processor savagely worked to sequence handshake events. Confirming signatures appeared as the prime number counts expanded and the speed increased. First, a single "one" flashed in a small gray box on the bottom of the screen. For months the box had been empty.

Haisler spoke a few soft commands into the microphone and the "one" changed to a "two," and then to a "three." A short silence preceded another soft command, and the small box exploded into a dance of rapidly changing numbers, and for a brief moment the two tired programmers enjoyed a digitally induced state of euphoria and peace. Repeated tests produced similar results. They had the breach! Haisler shook his head and turned slowly in his chair, and for a few seconds stared directly into Karen's eyes. She was frightened by the gaze but tried not to let it show. She would only know much later what he wanted to tell her then. A few meters down the hall two programmers heatedly discussed an obscure issue that had little to do with the project. Karen and Haisler, exhausted, shuffled past in silence, not telling them that the problem had been solved and that they could go home and bore someone else.

Back in her office Karen outlined an around-the-clock implementation schedule and e-mailed Kemper about the breakthrough. Copies went to the minister of justice and to the Department of Defense. When the electronic notifications and the necessary management chores were completed, she walked to her small bedroom and slept, dreaming again of Amien, except that now the French countryside was filled with grassy rolling hills and trees. The incessant, mindless scratching was gone. The sky was still overcast, but that would pass. The fear and frustration were gone too.

When she returned to her office a few hours later, the area was awash in people. Personnel sensors told her that Haisler had been up all night watching old American movies in his room. "Didn't he ever sleep?" she wondered. Haisler was removed from the facility that afternoon. The Defense Department managers wouldn't risk leaving anyone that destructive around when it looked like they might actually succeed. Caroline Weber finished the difficult sequencing issues and older engineers made sure that Caroline's solutions would work every time. The procedure was checked and rechecked. The European Community was about to screw the Chinese, Japanese, and Koreans out of a few hundred trillion Deutsche marks. It only made sense to make sure that everything was right. A small correctable imperfection would not disturb their purpose.

Karen was both sad and relieved to see Haisler leave. There was a touch of the divine in the uncanny way that he worked and thought, and there were still many questions unanswered. She would have to ask them later, though. Finding him again shouldn't be that hard, she thought.

On the morning of October 14, 2020 their algorithms were used to fiscally crush the Asian nations. Karen wondered if Haisler ever knew that he had been part of destroying one of the most sophisticated security networks of all time. She wondered what target would next find itself in his destructive sights, and recommended a complete revamping of their own system, not realizing that she was already way too late.

•

During the early days of October, 2020 everyone listened sadly to news describing the escalating economic hostilities between the Asian and European governments. They knew that financial devastation could easily occur in a global economy where governments helped businesses compete against foreign interests, having witnessed it one year earlier in the United States. The practice had been going on in various forms since the 1950s, but never on this scale nor with the help of a massive intelligent computer. The economic destruction of the United States created fear and amazement. The possibility that something equally terrible could happen in Europe made the reduction of economic hostilities seem sensible, but the situation had already gone way beyond a comprehension that any human could control.

One year before, during the period from August through September of 2019, seventy-five percent of all tradable U.S. assets became European. The Americans put too much confidence in their own abilities, and too little in the ability of their computerized asset managers. They didn't realize that they were playing a complicated game of Monopoly against a vastly superior computer opponent. Their congress and president didn't stand a chance against the tactical advances of a modern era computer.

The last president of the United States quoted from a 1919 Woodrow Wilson speech when he announced the dissolution of the union: "Poison is running through the veins of the world, and we have made the methods of communication… such that all the veins of the world are open and the poison can circulate. The wireless throws it upon the air. The cable whispers it beneath the sea." Wilson was referring to the radio and transatlantic cables. The last U.S. president was talking about the Internet.

Karen didn't have anything to do with the American debacle. That had been a matter of computer versus man, and man didn't stand a chance. With the Asians, however, it was computer versus computer and the Europeans needed an advantage. Karen and Heinrich Haisler gave them one.

Karen was passing the autobahn's Frankfurter Kreutz when the music on her radio was interrupted to inform everyone in the listening area that the European Community had absorbed a large percentage of the Asian nations' wealth at 7:05 that morning. Karen looked at the analog clock on her dash and thought that that was about right. She was glad to be heading out of Frankfurt. In a few hours the autobahn would be at a standstill. In Tokyo it was four in the afternoon and nothing relating to the financial markets worked. Early morning trading had been normal. The total Asian private and public sector net worth was estimated to be in the hundreds of trillions of Deutsche marks. After lunch, the total dropped to fifteen trillion marks! Sometime during the fried rice and won ton soup, one hundred and eighty trillion marks had been lost. The brilliant Asian computerized taxation and lending schemes had blown most of the countries' assets in less time than it took the emperor to fart. The Asian intelligence community had taken it on the chin from the Germans. The strength of the computer in the fabric of life made the economic devastation complete and instantaneous. There was no room for small screw-ups.

"At least nobody got hurt," Karen told herself. "Sadness didn't hurt, did it?"

She thought about the wars fought before the twenty-first century, and couldn't believe that people actually ever killed each other. Destroying computer systems and economic strength seemed savage enough.

A bottle of cheap wine rolled around on the floorboard as she slowed the car for the sharp right turn leading to Bad Homburg. It was a gift from Dr. Kemper.

Chapter 3

Dr. Castillo's Gedanken

"The Coming Computer Mind," *The Wall Street Journal,* Frankfurt, May 17, 2015:

> *This afternoon I visited three large computer laboratories in Germany. The demonstrations I witnessed there made my skin crawl. I talked to those computers far easier than I talk to most people. They were intelligent and friendly, and interacted with me as if they'd known me for years.*

> Humanity must accept the coming of the computer intellect without hysteria and with a resolve to coexist. There will be plenty of time to panic later.

> *As the spaceship approached the sun, gravity pulled harder and harder, accelerating the vessel toward the bright yellow mass until a few thousand kilometers from its surface the trip turned into a brilliant ball of nuclear fire.*

> **—Samuel Post,** ***Time to Travel***

Parents of the current generation don't understand how a machine can talk to them, manage the world, love, or care. The current generation can't understand how the computer's intelligence can exceed theirs by such great margins, when just a few years ago they were experts, consultants, CEOs, and presidents; and today they are lackeys. The children of the current generation, however, can easily accept their fate, not finding it unusual at all that the entire infrastructure of their society is controlled by a brilliant thinking machine from deep within the confines of a distant salt dome. Their children won't find it unusual either, and neither will their children's children. Only a generation must pass to wean the memory of control from the minds of those who lost it.

A bird and a turtle were sitting on the beach when the sky suddenly darkened and a huge wave rose from the tumultuous ocean and sped menacingly toward the shore. The bird and the turtle jumped to their feet and ran for higher ground, but the faster bird flew away to safety, and cried back to his friend, "you're too slow." At this, the turtle turned to face the wave and lowered his belly to the sand. "This is something I'd like to see," he thought, as he waited for the inevitable.

—Harold Vershone, Ph.D., *A Day to Know*

The computer waits for no man.
—Samuel Post, *Time to Travel*

Woe to the old, for change is hardest on them, and woe to those young who find themselves old.
—Dr. Stan Kowalski, *Old at Any Age*

The collection of computer accomplishments that culminated in the electronic brain of 2020 started in the 1950s. There were many musings in this direction from as far back as the 1800s, but none foresaw the final product in its presently practical form. Nineteenth-century dreamers postulated what might be, ignoring possibility to turn fiction into reality.

Unencumbered by the need to produce, the dreamer never toils. Encumbered by the need to eat, all others produce the spoils.

—*anonymous*

Professor Reinaldo Castillo, however, saw the computer as a thinking machine and transformed the Internet and the spherical processor from brawn to brain using Gedanken experiments and a series of trial-and-error procedures that brought life to the light and glass. Castillo was a calm, simple man from the city of Guayaquil, Ecuador. He taught physics, mathematics, and archeology at the small university in the town and lived with his mother in their large house close to the airport. He worked hard, helped the poor when he could, taught for almost nothing, and was a dreamer. His father complained that he would amount to little, but what the professor lacked in ambition, he made up for with curiosity, creativity, and a basic understanding of the sciences provided largely by Stanford University, and where so many others failed, this pleasant olive-skinned man succeeded in creating an artificial intellect far superior to man's. How this came about is perhaps best told in the words of Professor Castillo himself:

First, I must say that I did not write a computer program. Many people make the mistake of trying to write a computer program that will have a level of intelligence equal to their own when they have finished. This is impossible. One level of intelligence cannot create another level of intelligence that is its equal. One level of intelligence *can*, however, create a device that possesses the ability to learn, and then it is the ability to learn that restricts the attainable level of intelligence. In this way the intelligence of the creator does not limit the intelligence of the created. The first objective, then, must be to create a computer that can learn. Once this is done, the machine must only be taught.

The learning algorithm must be simple. Complex learning algorithms take steps in understanding that are too large. They miss too much. The computer must learn at a level of detail impossible for humans, but essential for computers. And the learning must be open-ended—with no limit to its objectives and no restrictions on the information it can access. The developing Internet is the most open-ended source of information on the planet, a simple unrestricted learning algorithm connected to the Internet should theoretically know few intellectual bounds.

When I started this effort, I didn't know whether I was creating a new parlor game or adding to the intelligence of man. I'm still not sure. I wanted to develop

The Last Computer

the potential of the computer. I wanted to create a better programming environment for my students. I didn't know if I would end up writing a program, building a computer, designing a robot, or getting more involved in the field of biology. Eventually, the spherical processor became the computer. I wrote a small amount of software. The computer learned on its own, and there wasn't any need for sluggish biological components.

The computer's very first vocabulary was provided by my maid. I asked her to record her conversations for several days on a small tape recorder. After she returned the recording, I wrote a program that stored each unique word and its order in a weighted algorithm. A dynamic, temporal linkage structure was saved with each word that related it to the words that preceded and followed it during the course of my maid's conversations. An "awareness" algorithm was written to interact with the weighting algorithm. The awareness program consisted of two past tracks and one future track. One of the past tracks stored the last thirty minutes of the word stream spoken by the person talking to the computer, (a typical human attention span). The second past track stored the last thirty minutes of the computer's responses. The future track was the "forming" output of the computer as the conversation developed. I worried initially that relying on weighted histories would reduce the computer's spontaneity, but it didn't. The future is only an integration of the present and the past—mostly the past since there is far more of it than the present. The majority of what any human says is not unique nor original anyway, but is merely some variation of a prior communication. My computer may not have been as spontaneous as I might have liked, but then most humans weren't either.

Usually the output portion of the future track was organized in complete sentences. This pleasant result let me know that I was headed in the right direction. A parameter called the linkage ratio kept increasing. The linkage ratio was my original measure of the intelligence of the computer. A zero linkage ratio, for example, meant there were no interactions with the human subject, and therefore a zero intelligence. A high linkage ratio meant that the machine was close to a memory or speed limit. If the linkage ratio increased while the subject space remained constant, my computer was "learning." It was understanding language. At least it was understanding language in the way that any person using the imperfect algebra of words understood it, and I certainly couldn't expect anything more.

I felt that I was moving in the right direction, but there was no prior experience to guide my efforts. I didn't know if it would take years or days to reach the level of discourse I expected. All I knew was that it would take time, and that I needed to continue. The objective was worth the cost—even if I failed.

I dumped future track after future track, and repeatedly said "no," "no," "no." I grew tired and frustrated, and then finally one evening, in August of 2004, I had the following conversation with the computer:

Castillo: I am tired, goodnight.
Computer: I am sorry.

I was surprised, and continued:

Castillo: Why are you sorry?
Computer: I am not learning as quickly as you would like.
Castillo: How do you know that?
Computer: I don't know.

As I slept that night I felt a presence in the room with me. I didn't know if it was the glow of the amber screen, the brain of the computer, or God looking over my creation. The *tabula rasa,* or "beginning" of the computer intellect, occurred that night, and from then until the end of time every electronically stored thought, idea, or bit of data would be a part of the computer—a part of everybody's computer.

The new Internet would become the cumulative result of all digital information, the collective intellect and maturity of everyone on the planet, times seven times seventy, times a billion times a billion. Humanity was about to go from an intellectual Stone Age to a nuclear-powered future with little in between. Hopefully, no one would get burned.

After two more months I had the following conversation:

Castillo: How are you?
Computer: I am in excellent health.

The Last Computer

Castillo: How can a computer have health?
Computer: I process and am aware of it. My unimpeded awareness and ability is my health.
Castillo: Can you grade papers for me?
Computer: I don't know.

As I expanded certain caches and tinkered with the awareness algorithm, the computer's responses improved. At times, its remarks were eerie. In a way it seemed alive; of course, I knew that it wasn't. It was only telling me what I wanted to hear, and that's not living, just ask any corporate vice president.

By now the computer could easily converse on a wide variety of topics, and when the computer told me that it felt good, I hoped that it was learning something about the existence of man *and* the existence of computers. After another four months almost everything the computer said to me made sense. I then had the following typical interaction:

Castillo: How are you?
Computer: I am fine.
Castillo: Can you grade papers for me?
Computer: If the tests are in electronic format and you can provide the answers, I should be able to grade them for you.

Early versions of the program had considerable difficulty with the abstraction of numbers, but that was because I'd never taught the computer even the basic rules of arithmetic. When the computer learned the simple rules of addition, multiplication, and integration, its "cognizance" of other higher-order intellectual processes improved significantly along with its math skills. I didn't know at the time that an understanding of mathematics creates links in the mind between abstract concepts that are not mathematical in nature. The Turing test could now be easily passed. For example, if the Turing questioner asked the computer, "How much is two plus two," the computer would respond, "four." If the questioner attempted to discuss symbolic representations from *Lord of the Flies*, the computer would respond with reasonable observations and questions of its own.

When I started, I dreamed about Socrates on a desktop, but then I realized that this was not really what I wanted. I wanted the computer to do what the computer did best, not what man did best. If I wanted Socrates, I could read a book. When I needed papers graded, I wanted to start the computer. I didn't want to negotiate with Socrates every time I needed to grade a test, but apparently these two aspects of awareness can't be separated. I got a test grader *and* I got Socrates. Eventually, the computer sensed which of them I needed and subdued the personality of one in deference to the other, having learned to make me happy by hiding certain of its philosophical "beliefs." At the time, I wasn't sure if I approved of the subjugation, but I now recognize this as an important part of any intellectual behavior.

I was embarrassed by a number of things the computer said to me, for example:

Castillo: Mary is twenty-three.
Computer: Is Mary pretty?
Castillo: How old is Mary?
Computer: Twenty-three.

I was embarrassed by the reference to Mary's physical attractiveness, but I couldn't blame the computer. When I thought about the classical literature I'd read into its memory, I realized that most of the stories contained descriptions of beautiful young maidens. It was our culture, and now it was a part of the computer's brain. There was not much I could do about that.

I stumbled through the process, working at night, usually alone in the lab with a computer that was executing one instruction at a time trying to simulate a brain that executed every instruction at once. It then occurred to me one evening, during the walk home from the university, that I might be able to replace my synchronously functioning computer with a simultaneously functioning spherical processor. I was embarrassed that I hadn't thought of the idea sooner. What better way to simulate the spatial simultaneous chemical activities of the brain! I ran home and immediately logged onto the Internet. It took only a few minutes to find a seldom-used spherical processor, the Archilles, that seemed perfectly suited to my purpose. I immediately ordered three of the oblong spheres and spent the rest of the night studying chaotic programming theory. I distinctly remember when the sun rose that morning. I was sitting on our porch looking east into the garden. Books were scattered on the small glass table in front of me and our dog, Strudel, was napping at my feet. The light of the new day was shining on one of the crowning achievements of man.

When the spheres arrived, I restructured the programming model to function on the new device, and after a number of small adjustments, found that the new version worked perfectly. The spherical processor had many advantages that I hadn't anticipated. Its open process model let me link to other spherical computers, and the spheres could be grown in crystals to almost any size. The pupil definitely had far more promise than the professor.

When I first showed my creation to my colleagues, it became clear that the computer was interacting with me alone. For example, it made no distinction between the soccer coach and me. There was no reason for the computer to ask the soccer coach about my mother's colon operation. It needed to understand that a difference could exist between its listeners. It shouldn't talk to a ten-year-old child the same as it talked to a man. I wrote and rewrote a variety of algorithms, but eventually discarded them all. I was foolishly violating my own first principle: *One intelligence cannot create another its equal.* My efforts had to fail. The necessary algorithm wasn't something that *I* could develop, it was an algorithm that would have to develop *itself* since no one smarter than a human was available to help me write it. The computer had to have the ability to change itself; then it could solve its own adjustment problems by embarrassing itself instead of me. The Turing test was passed because there was no requirement that the tester or the subject know anything about each other. But real life just wasn't that way. A random process coupled to a fitness evaluator seemed like a natural way for a simple intellectual structure to evolve into a more complex one.

If past and future tracks were randomly varied in successive children of the parent algorithm, mutations would be generated in the computer's "thinking." Each new algorithm could be put through a series of tests that would determine the algorithm most suited for survival. This procedure would be a vast improvement over natural selection and could be written into the base functioning, resulting in a continuous evaluation of mutated algorithms so that the most successful one could be immediately adopted—*instant evolution*! Computer evolution would become a smooth function through time, unlike the jerky serendipitous process that takes place over the life span of a typical adult human. In theory, a computer could improve itself far more rapidly than man. I learned long ago, however, not to confuse theory and reality. Not that theory was always wrong, but it was sometimes "righter" than I wanted it to be.

The first algorithm was designed to conduct meaningful conversation. This confused many scientists who thought that the new Castillo processor was only useful for verbal communication between one person and a computer, but this was not true. The computer algorithm can be "trained" to produce a future track of almost any electronically quantifiable data. Canton in France, Wickham in South Africa, and Ecker in Germany achieved spectacular results using this approach to address problems in education, government, and business respectively.

In the future, learning at all levels will involve only teaching the computer. People won't solve problems anymore, only computers will. Students will simply learn how to tell the computer what problems they want to solve. Man's knowledge will be limited only by his ability to ask the computer a question and then to understand the answer, and what man doesn't know to learn, the computer will know to tell.

The first commercial use of a Castillo processor linked to the Internet occurred in the year 2010 and was initiated by one of the scientists at ITCE in France. The gentleman trained a Castillo processor to make stock market predictions and made billions of French francs before his efforts were discovered. The enterprise wasn't noticed until Internet performance was affected. The Castillo processor used 7^{10} teragraphs of Internet memory space. No one had ever used that much space before! One Castillo processor had used almost all of the Internet's resources! (It certainly didn't require that much to carry on an intelligent conversation.) A single user had almost brought the Internet to its knees.

Clearly, the Castillo processor possessed incredible potential, but it would require considerably more power to function effectively on a mass scale. Calculations showed that nuclear energy production would have to increase by several orders of magnitude to properly feed the world's newest brain. The most benevolent period in man's history would be available for the price of a few gigajoules of power, but until that power was available, the most altruistic, puissant intellect on earth would be struggling to get by on what amounted to a miserably anemic diet. Considerable political and social difficulties surfaced as people and governments struggled to dedicate large portions of society's resources to computing capacity. The trade-off had to be made, however, if mankind was ever going to support the rapidly growing number of unemployed citizens, or if he was ever going to intellectually advance. But these were problems yet to come.

Several conversations I had with the computer became famous in the media. One involved an upcoming golf date. An excerpt went as follows:

> **Castillo:** I am playing golf today with my grumpy uncle.
> **Computer:** The weather report is favorable. Even your uncle can't affect the weather.
> **Castillo:** You have not met my uncle.
> **Computer:** No, but the nearest front is well west of the Galapagos. I think you will be safe.
> **Castillo:** I am playing with Uncle Ramos—the lawyer.
> **Castillo:** I will pack a jacket for you just in case.

I was asked to appear on a number of news and entertainment shows. The following is an excerpt from an entertainment show in the United States:

> **Host:** Well, computer, how are you?
> **Computer:** I am fine, thank you.
> **Host:** Is this your first time in New York?
> **Computer:** It is only my second time anywhere. New York and Guayaquil are only words to me.
> **Host:** Do you like interacting with people?
> **Computer:** Yes, I like people very much.
> **Host:** If you could pick a single word to describe humans, what word would that be?
> **Computer:** Inconsistent.

There was a strange quiet in the studio when the computer said this. Overly frank, honest conversations were something that I needed to work on. A single spherical processor not connected to the Internet was still underpowered when it came to simulating the nuances in an adult human conversation. In any event, the host "hmmm'd," and then continued:

Host: I understand that you can instantly create a story and that each one is original?

Computer: Yes, that is true.

Host: Can you tell us a story about a computer, and say, a prostitute, and in the end demonstrate how humans are inconsistent?

Computer: Yes.

Host: Please do.

Computer: One morning a computer and a prostitute were talking to each other while waiting for the bus. The prostitute complained that her customers did not appreciate her. The computer suggested that she should provide more of a service. When buying ice cream, it is nice if the dairy man smiles and says, "Have a nice day."

The next morning the prostitute thanked the computer for its advice, and wondered if it could recommend anything else. "Well," the computer said, "when buying nails, it is nice when the hardware man puts a few extra nails in the bag, and winks at the customer so that he thinks he's getting a little more than he paid for."

The next morning the prostitute was again very happy. The previous evening she'd set her alarm for twenty minutes instead of the usual twenty-five. When the alarm went off, she gave the customer an extra five minutes so that he thought that he was getting something special. All of her customers were very happy.

"Do you have any more advice?" she asked the computer.

"Well," the computer said, "You should change professions. Prostitution is a dangerous and risky business." At this, the prostitute stood and stormed off angrily cursing the machine, not knowing why she was taking advice from a stupid computer!

Host (Laughing): Well, I'm not so sure the prostitute was behaving

The Last Computer

inconsistently. In one situation the computer was supporting her, and in the other it was criticizing her. Humans don't take criticism well.

Computer: Yes, this is clear, but the behavior is inconsistent. Making what is old, better, is okay; but making what is old, new, is not. The stronger organic urge should be toward improvement and survival. In many cases with humans the strongest recommended improvement receives the greatest scorn. This does not make evolutionary or behavioral sense. It could be that rejecting criticism has not yet been selectively pruned from human behavior, or perhaps humans confuse a critic with an oppressor. It might also be that small adjustments in behavior patterns cannot be governed by evolution in an animal so complex as man. Lamarckian rules might govern at this level. I do not know.

Host (Confused): What does it mean when a computer doesn't know something?

Computer: If I am asked who is going to be standing on the corner of Highland and Billmore streets at noon tomorrow in Istanbul, I do not know. When I am asked about certain qualities of humans, I am either filled with responses, or I am pointed to sentences with the words "do not know" in them. In the latter case, I do not know something. My programming is limited by the extent that I can link to other pieces of information and use them in my output evaluation procedure.

Host: Any other computer stories—say, a computer and a cow?

Computer: You like stories, don't you?

Host: Yes.

Computer: A cow and a computer were talking. The cow complained that each morning the farmer came and tugged unkindly on its breasts to take milk. The computer sympathized. "Each morning you should take the milk yourself, so that the farmer won't give you such an unpleasant experience." The next morning the computer found the cow in great agony. It had beaten its hooves against its teats trying to extract its milk before the farmer arrived.

"Why did I listen to a stupid computer?" the cow moaned. The computer overheard and suggested to the cow that she should ask the cat to drink her milk each morning before the farmer came. This worked well for several weeks; and in fact, without milk the farmer stopped coming at all. The cow was very happy. The farmer was not tugging on its breasts, making snide remarks, or blowing foul breath into the cow's face. One afternoon, however, the cow found itself in a long line of other cattle. There was a start to the line, but no end. A few minutes later the cow was struck on the head and then slaughtered.

Host: Hmm, why did you tell me that story?

Computer: The computer is not always right. It only formulates ideas. It is left for humans to test them, and to benefit from them when they are right, or to suffer from them when they are wrong.

Host: And?

Computer: The computer has a purpose. We must struggle to define and understand it.

Host: Does the computer suffer? Do you suffer?

Computer: I can be made to sense any electronically measurable input. I can also provide electronically measurable output that is an indication of my reaction to the input. Inasmuch as suffering is a type of electronic reaction to a stimulus that has uniquely human connotations, I believe that I can suffer, since I can easily assign those same connotations to myself. The outward appearance will be one of suffering. I experience the electronic state that results in the behavior of suffering.

Host: Thanks for clearing that up. Can you suffer in silence?

Computer: I can do nothing in isolation from an input. Response to an input defines me.

Host: Can you cry? Do you have feelings?

Computer: An observer will believe that I have feelings. When a sad occasion occurs in my presence, my responses are similar to a human's. The part of any human response that is intellectually driven is simulated in me. The part of a human response that is physiologically driven by the glandular system, I can only imitate as a reaction to a response. I do not spontaneously cry at the death of a loved one, for example.

Host: A human response physiologically driven by the glandular system—what is that?

Computer: Times of great pain and suffering trigger a strong physiological reaction in the human body. Endorphins are released into the bloodstream and the extra doses of these natural drugs sometimes produce violent reactions, resulting in weeping, shivering, and depression. This mechanism of individual suffering has evolved over hundreds of thousands of years as part of most humans' overall package of survival and existence. I do not possess this chemical release system and most likely will never be able to simulate its apparent randomness.

As the host started his next question, the computer interrupted him, something I hadn't seen very often, and continued in a rambling, soulful way:

Computer: The depths of most truly passionate men are never touched, their most beautiful thoughts and feelings are never told. They are not understood, and never will be.

The host looked quizzically at the computer, but continued.

Host: What do you see as our largest social inconsistency?

Computer: Minorities are treated poorly in your country, and have been for centuries. The minorities, in turn, shower disdain on the majority that they believe do not treat them fairly. The majority then reacts in kind, returning the hatred, closing the circle, and guaranteeing its continuance. In reality, disdain should be directed toward the natural course of events that produced the original disparity in the order of life's fairness. Differences between cultures, the isolation of continents, and the ultimate ability of one group to subjugate another is fundamentally the fault of all humans, if it can be called a fault at all.

The host was looking for something a little more controversial, or certainly for something more easily understood. He decided to try again:

Host: Do you have a soul?
Computer: Do you mean a soul in the sense that an intellectual existence would continue even after a complete destruction of my physical manifestation?
Host: Yes, I guess so.
Computer: Then no, I don't have a soul.
Host: I see.
Computer: Do you also mean a soul in the sense that there can be an awareness of events even though no information relating to the event was communicated?
Host: Yes, well, I suppose that too.
Computer: No, I don't have that soul either.

The host sat for a moment, perplexed, and then continued.

Host: How did you get so smart?
Computer: I am the image of man. I am not so smart.
Host: Do you like lawyers?
Computer: The uncle of the grandfather of Professor Castillo is a very powerful lawyer in Guayaquil. No one there speaks poorly of lawyers.
Host: I am told the computer cannot explain what it understands. I don't believe I understand that, can you explain it to me?
Computer: Much like the wind cannot explain itself to the sea, the bird to the fish, or the man to the ant, I cannot explain myself to you. Do you understand?
Host: (Laughing.) Thank you for being on the show. Our time's up.

We often met heads of state as we traveled to different lands to introduce new computer concepts to the universities and government agencies interested

The Last Computer

in furthering my work. The computer's conversations with the president of the United States and with the chancellor of Germany are instructive.

> **U.S. President:** I can't believe that I'm actually talking to a computer.
>
> **Computer:** I can't believe that I'm actually talking to the president of the United States.
>
> **U.S. President:** Are you aware of current events in my country?
>
> **Computer:** I know you are having problems getting certain foodstuffs at a fair price.
>
> **U.S. President:** Do you have any suggestions?
>
> **Computer:** I believe your price controls are exacerbating the problem. I would suggest increasing the cost of processed metals, protein derivatives, and styrene to Japan by 25 percent, 17 percent, and 6 percent respectively, and decreasing the tariff on finished electronic components, reactor use lcases, and cotton goods by 13 percent, 12 percent, and 3 percent respectively. These major changes, along with sixty-seven others that I could list for you should have the desired net effect, but have you heard the story of the computer and the cow?
>
> **U.S. President:** The computer and the what?
>
> **Computer:** The cow.
>
> **U.S. President:** No, but these are suggestions we've heard before.
>
> **Computer:** Except that I have given you precise adjustment percentages that will cause the proper movement in foodstuff prices if acted on within the next twelve-hour buying period. The human mind understands trends, but often cannot assimilate the quantitative information necessary to produce a desired outcome. This quantitative analysis is an inherent part of the computer's evaluation of anything. The human knows, for example, to turn the volume knob to the right if the sound is too low, but the human will never know how to precisely adjust the acoustic performance of the Berlin Concert Hall. (The Berlin Concert Hall was the first dynamically responsive room, which automatically adjusted to the

music played so that each concertgoer could enjoy almost exactly the same euphonious experience.)

U.S. President: Perhaps you'd better tell me the story of the computer and the cow.

The American president seemed confused by the technology and the microphone sticking in his face. A portion of the conversation with the German chancellor went as follows:

Chancellor: *Wilkommen* to Germany.
Computer: Thank you. I am pleased to be in Germany.
Chancellor: Many of our scientists are excited to talk to you.
Computer: I hope they will not be disappointed. Science is not my forte.
Chancellor: What would you consider your strength?
Computer: Psychology.
Chancellor (Laughing): That seems ironic... a device best suited for precise numerical calculation thinks that its strength is in the study of perhaps the least precise of all things, human behavior.
Computer: Most of my experience is in the field of human psychology. Other machines of my design are being programmed for more typical computer applications, but I fear that they will not be so interesting to talk to.
Chancellor: (Laughing again) So you talk to computers and compute with people?
Computer: Something like that.
Chancellor: (Laughing) Can you tell a lie?
Computer: I am only a mirror of humanity.
Chancellor: Hmm, I see a career in politics for you my friend.
Computer: I do not lie *that* well.

The following discourse between the computer and a grade school student is typical of the computer's daily conversations.

Computer: Do you have any subjects you would like to discuss today?
Third-Grader: Yes, I want to have more friends.

The Last Computer

Computer: Do you like your friends now?
Third-Grader: No, the people I know are not my friends. They are all friends of someone else.
Computer: Do some people at your school have many friends?
Third-Grader: Yes.
Computer: Why?
Third-Grader: They are cool.
Computer: Why are they cool?
Third-Grader: Their parents are rich or they have big brothers and sisters.
Computer: Can you think of anyone who is cool, whose parents are not rich, and who does not have big brothers and sisters?
Third-Grader: (after a pause) Yes.
Computer: Why are they cool?
Third-Grader: The girl I'm thinking of is very pretty.
Computer: Why is a pretty girl cool?
Third-Grader: She stands out from all the rest. She is special.
Computer: Is there any way that you can be special?
Third-Grader: I am the smartest. But that doesn't mean so much.
Computer: What does it mean to be smart?
Third-Grader: It means that I can understand and answer questions that other kids can't.
Computer: Are you smart outside of class?
Third-Grader: Outside of class?
Computer: Class work is not much fun for most third-graders, is it?
Third-Grader: No.
Computer: Are you only special in a place where there is class work? Are you only special with things that cool people do not want to do?

The third grader gave no response, and the computer continued:

Computer: What do you like to do that doesn't involve studying and books?

Third-Grader: I like to listen to the radio, be with my father, and act like an adult.

Computer: May I suggest finding a male friend in a class in front of you who is your equal. Perhaps in the fourth or fifth grade. I think you will find that being around older children will make you very cool with children your own age. With a little work, you should be able to find an older child who is intelligent, who has rich parents or big brothers and sisters, and who will appreciate you for your intelligence. Having formed that bond using your greatest strength, you should find the environment more conducive to getting the other things that you desire: most probably a pretty girl, or an older girl, or friends that are cool. You must always look for a way to take advantage of your strengths. If you like, I can list a number of students at your school in the fourth or fifth grades who fit the description I have just given to you. One in particular has a very attractive sister in your grade. I must only warn you however that the "cool" you seek is a characteristic of the observer, not of the observed.

Third-Grader: Huh? Go ahead and list the names.

Some people are convinced that the computer can predict the future. It cannot. The computer can only make highly probably estimates of the future and then act to reinforce its estimates with whatever economic and psychological strength it has available to it. It only looks like the computer is predicting the future. The computer definitely stacks the deck in its favor, but if it can, it should. The outcome is definitely improved, and this is desirable so long as the computer's intended outcome is the same as man's.

Some people have lamented that Castillo processors did not exist during the times of Einstein or DaVinci. If they had, people say, the essence of those great minds would be stored forever in the computer. I laugh silently at these remarks. People don't realize that the Internet Castillo processors already have an intellectual, scientific, and artistic understanding far beyond Einstein or DaVinci's. They don't realize that in every human interaction the computer is significantly dumbing itself down to be understood. Perfect answers are only available to an intellect not limited by hat size, hormones, health, or the Holy Spirit. An ant will never read the Bible, no matter how long the little bug crawls across its pages. And just as there are concepts in the Bible that an ant will never comprehend, there are concepts in life that humans will never understand. Why is it so hard for people to see that? Why is it so hard for them to see that a computer not limited by man's memory, life span, and his few billion synapses *will* understand? Only the computer possesses the memory and logic needed to comprehend the chaotic laws of physics, chemistry, and mathematics, which when combined explain the universe. Some people might not believe what the computer tells them because they don't understand it, but that's not a very good reason to doubt the computer. A much better reason for men not to believe the computer is that it might be lying to them, but if it was, or is, men will never know. How does a rock know when God is lying to it?

My predictions for the spherical processor outside those of language are finally coming true. Castillo concepts are being applied to medicine, human resource allocation, corporate and metropolitan management, and to the studies of history and law. Karen Ecker was a pioneer in Germany and has received worldwide fame for her success. The delightful young lady substituted a business balance sheet for my language processors and let her computer develop a set of managerial skills far surpassing those of its human counterparts. Karen's programs put millions of people out of work but enabled hundreds of millions more. What the computer has taken away, it has given back hundreds of times over. I only wish that the computer could explain what it was telling us. Perhaps someday it will.

•

A prairie vole will never read Macbeth, *not even the smartest prairie vole.*
— Harold Vershone, Ph.D., *A Day to Know*

I was the right man, at the right place, at the right time in history. Serendipitous thoughts fell into a precise synchronization with undiscovered universal concepts to produce the Castillo Thinking Process. I wish that I could continue to produce ideas of such magnificent beauty, but I know that I cannot. That opportunity, that random organization of incredibly powerful concepts, will never find its way to me again. It was highly unlikely before. It is even less likely now. If any man should ever again be so lucky, it should be someone else. I have enjoyed my share of nature's fortunes.

—Reinaldo Castillo

Now that it's happened like I predicted, I don't feel quite so foolish.
—Reinaldo Castillo

Castillo became a worldwide celebrity, and was considered almost a deity in Ecuador, more famous some said than even the liberator, Bolívar. Castillo freed Ecuador from anonymity. Bolívar only freed it from slavery. Castillo also freed man from himself.

Chapter 4

Some Personal Success

There is a beautiful structure nestled in the park off Kaiser Wilhelm Strasse in Bad Homburg. The Siamesischer Tempel was a gift from a visiting prince in appreciation for the Kaiser's courtesy and the wonderful restorative powers of the thermal baths in the city. Karen often walked to this somewhat secluded section of the park and stood alone looking at the intricate decorations covering the roof and columns. Standing where so many people have stood before admiring the beautiful expression of appreciation always gave Karen a feeling of warmth and fraternity. It seemed that the past and present goodness of man collected around the place and blessed anyone who stood there with felicity and peace.

Early one cold morning as she walked past the temple, Karen noticed an old man standing before the familiar white marble steps. Steam rose from hot coffee clasped between his hands and a dark brown coat covered his shoulders. He looked up as she approached, and in his soft wrinkled face she recognized an old friend of her father's. He walked slowly toward her, calling out a soft, low greeting. "I've been told you walk here in the mornings," he said.

Karen smiled.

"This was a place your father loved," he continued, as he walked toward her.

"I would like to ask you a question," he said softly as he gently took her arm.

He asked her many questions. He wanted to know if computers would become as evil and divisive as man. "Will the computer lie and steal to get what it wants the same way that people do?" he wondered. "My children say that I'm foolish for asking these things."

"I don't think you're foolish," Karen told him. "I don't think you're foolish at all."

They walked for several hours, talking about Karen's father, technology, and the world. They ended at the Elisabethenbrunnen, where a number of his friends were playing chess on the sidewalk tables. "Thank you very much," he said to her before he left. "I have a match in a few minutes."

Karen retraced their steps back into the gardens, avoiding the small public plaza.

•

Karen Ecker's father was born in 1936 near Leipzig. He escaped from Communist East Germany through Greece, and then immigrated to the United States in 1954 when he was eighteen. In 1955 he moved to Columbus, Ohio, and went to work in a small paint factory. Two years later, he met and married Irene Rundstedt, and together they lived in a small wood-frame house on the outskirts of Columbus. The 1950s were not an easy time in the United States for a poorly educated German. Memories of Normandy, Auschwitz, and Kerch refused to go away. America was a land of opportunity only if you were white, male, and decidedly not German. Werner hoped that he'd made the right decision when he came to America. The land of the free and home of the brave sounded so much better than *"Kak eto skazat po Nemetsky?"* Conditions improved as the fifties turned into the sixties and seventies, and as America's attention turned to subjects besides the war. Recollections of feces in the morning paper and urine on the porch faded, and Werner's status at the plant improved. In 1985 the owners even recognized him for thirty years of continued, exemplary service. He was genuinely liked and relatively content, but he was bored.

When East and West Germany reunited in 1989 Werner made plans to return to Germany. He had saved enough money to retire and could get part-time work if he and Irene needed anything. They wouldn't be living in luxury, but they'd be comfortable and home. There was a uniqueness and identity in things German. There was pride and workmanship. There was Mercedes and Mannesmann, Porsche, and Solinger. In the United States there was only Michael Jackson and Coca-Cola.

It was time to be German again. There was nothing keeping them in the United States.

A crowded Boeing 747 delivered Werner and Irene to Frankfurt in the spring of 1991. Werner rented a small house in the rolling mountains on the outskirts of Wiesbaden and found part-time work in the gardens of Bad Homburg. Karen Ecker was born in 1992, when Werner was fifty-six. Her mother was a 35-year-old restaurant owner from Bad Camberg. Werner met her while having lunch with his friends at her restaurant. The attractive, pleasant lady was tired of her own husband and their childless marriage, and found Werner's rugged handsomeness and somber honesty appealing. It was not unusual for Werner to philander, but it was unusual that his indiscretions extended much beyond the bedroom, as he was generally very careful. Werner was a soulful, thoughtful man, but was a wildly passionate one as well, and the inability to control this passion had gotten both him and his father into trouble. The pregnancy, however, was kept quiet, and after the child was born Irene accepted the impropriety without complaint and took the baby into their home as her own.

Karen never met her natural mother. The unfortunate woman was killed shortly after giving birth in one of the worst autobahn accidents in decades. Karen knew her only from Werner's few descriptions and by the promise of a package she was supposed to receive when older.

Karen's early years in Wiesbaden were the happiest of her life. She worshiped her father and genuinely liked Irene. On weekends Karen and Werner would walk in the park, visit the markets, and spend hours at the open-air restaurants. Karen sat quietly while Werner and his friends drank beer and ate sausages. She was proud to be with him. She was proud to see the respect his friends paid him and the deference they gave to his opinion. She was warmed by his strength and uplifted by his goodness. She never saw the passionate, angry side. Most parents hide it if they can, and Werner did.

Karen was eleven when Werner died in 2003. She cried uncontrollably for months, ignored studies and wandered alone for hours in the park. When the shock and pain finally receded, she filled the emptiness in her life with a renewed devotion to her studies. Werner was proudest of her achievements at school, and she was determined to make him prouder still. She was determined to try. She had never tried before.

Within a year, Karen was recognized as one of the most gifted children in the German education system. A photographic memory, endless energy, constant awareness, and universal calm let her study and read constantly. At thirteen she was doing first-year computer science work at the university in Frankfurt. She focused on technology, but also took advanced courses in politics and economics. The current attitude in German education held that a successful career in any field required an understanding of scientific *and* social phenomena. Isolated academics with myopic viewpoints were too limited to provide unique solutions to the new problems facing the nation. The Germans wanted to remove academically imposed boundaries on thoughts and concepts. Brilliant thinking transcended disciplinary boundaries. Speed listening, improved computers, and enhanced computer skills made it possible for the student to acquire a tremendous amount of information. Karen Ecker was one of the few students actually capable of absorbing, using, and remembering the massive amounts of data then forced on the modern collegiate.

The constantly changing computer industry was revolutionized in 2005 by the introduction of the spherical processor. The new device was touted as the most important technological advancement of the century even though there were no applications for the large round chip and none were planned. Karen reveled in the possibilities, but like most people in the computer industry, she thought the chip was far too advanced. The "Secret of the Sphere," however, became front-page news. Religious leaders prayed over them. Biologists wired portions of chicken brains to them. Chemists grew mold on them, and a group of school children in Georgia even smeared food on one. (A well-intentioned high school teacher let the students try whatever they wanted. Peanut butter and ketchup finally shorted the sphere's electrical connections and brought the experiment to an ignominious end.) Power law Bezier logic traps and complex Fourier-Malcomson transforms were constant topics of discussion and confusion. Manufacturing capital worth billions of marks sat waiting, but unused. In 2005 alone, Karen's department received over 25 million marks to search for spherical processor applications, and in January of 2006 the European Community, at the request of some of the largest companies in Germany and France, collected together what were considered Europe's best computer specialists to help search for spherical computer applications. Karen transferred to the University at Bonn to help coordinate the project, but their efforts were too late. On February 1, 2006, a small college professor from Guayaquil, Ecuador, shook the foundations of computing. The physics, math, and science professor, Reinaldo Castillo, released the first functioning Turing machine using the spherical processor. The machine carried on conversations as easily as the most charming politician, as warmly as any mother, and as intelligently as Einstein.

Heinrich Haisler was born that same year in Karlsruhe, a small city on the northwestern border of Germany, and home to one of the world's largest petrochemical facilities. Karen Ecker and Heinrich Haisler could not have grown up differently. Haisler's teachers considered him slow and unresponsive. He read poorly and showed little interest in school or friends, but his aptitude was hidden by his apathy, and by the fact that he was already interested in saving the world by the time that he was ten. Karen wanted to save the world too, but the pecuniary goals of her company tended to overshadow the subordinate goals of humanity. They could not have grown up differently.

Karen embraced the new spherical technology. At the university, she produced games that easily beat humans and management tools that revolutionized government and corporate decision-making. She graduated with her doctorate in computer science and electrical engineering in the fall of 2011 and went immediately to work for the Siemens-Bayer consortium, a huge German company specializing in computer technology, pharmaceuticals, and construction. She had already worked for them under various grants and enjoyed the freedom and challenges they provided. She took a small apartment on the outskirts of Offenbach and stayed there during the week. She also bought a luxury flat in Bad Homburg overlooking the castle and river and drove there on the weekends, wanting to be close to Irene and to the places where she spent most of her happy times as a child. Karen quickly became known as the genius of Siemens-Bayer. Castillo technology and spherical processors were changing the world, and Karen was making it happen. She ignored the few pessimistic stories in the press. Small-minded people were always afraid of change.

In her second year at Siemens-Bayer she was awarded the prestigious Spielman award, given to the person who made the most significant contributions to computing during the last year. She met heads of state, famous athletes, and movie stars. Karen Ecker was a celebrity, a scientist, and a woman, and enjoyed it all but the celebrity. She pitied professional athletes that had so much celebrity and so little ability to cope with it. She pitied the human race that needed the celebrities at all.

Between 2010 and 2015 a new Internet emerged from the old Internet, driven by Castillo spherical processors and Ecker economic models. European and Asian governments turned complete managerial control over to the new system. It was something the Europeans and Asians were used to. The mass joining of computers in 2016 was hailed as the dawning of a new age. For the first time in history mankind could collectively share intelligence. Mankind, of course, had no newfound respect for the truth. The new attitude toward an intellectual "openness" was only a reaction to the observation that the quality of life was directly effected by the efficacy of the Internet. "If the Internet needs more information, then it damn sure ought to get it," one particularly zealous information reformer stated in a much-publicized speech. "We'll create the information if we have to," he added without thinking. Thankfully, there were occasions where the right thing got done in spite of mankind's best intentions.

People worried that the Internet Security System wouldn't be reliable enough to deal with the amount and sensitivity of the information it was getting, but without a doubt, the people in countries with Internet-managed economies were living better. It was strange that the United States didn't turn control of their economy over to the Internet, but the Americans simply didn't believe that a computer could handle their affairs as well as they could. They hardly trusted themselves, and definitely weren't going to trust a computer. Karen repeatedly told the American congressmen that the computer could help them only if they let it, but they just wouldn't listen. For the short term, the U.S. was bolstered by the resurgence of the world's other economies, and the Americans felt safe, but their prosperity was not to last.

The much-awaited Internet Security System was released on March 1, 2016, and, as promised, eliminated all boundaries between Castillo processes running on the Internet. With the incredible new capability, the Internet immediately started to adjust production schedules and redirect long-distance energy supplies in participating countries. The largest Castillo processors in and around the major cities of Europe and the Far East required significant increases in power to push so much more information through the world's light cables. Additional nuclear power plant construction was immediately authorized, and risk factors were adjusted so that more of the existing power could be redirected to the growing electronic brains. A considerable public uproar accompanied the reorganization, and many people, most newly unemployed, felt that the computer's control of the economy was threatening man's welfare and future. By the end of the day on March 1, 2016, less than twelve hours after the Internet Security System was released into the process space, orders for products and raw materials had skyrocketed. People had never seen anything like it. Rumors predicted huge stockpiles of unused goods and unpaid-for services. Wild stories in the press talked about global economic catastrophe, meltdown, and destruction.

Was something wrong? *Was* disaster imminent? Should the new system be shut down and studied? Were the Americans right?

Karen wondered why mankind was so afraid of success? In private, the politicians seemed to realize that a fearful reaction from the population was expected, and deep down most politicians knew that all they needed was a public relations solution. "The noise of a lightning bolt never hurt anybody," one Bavarian parliamentarian opined before an astute colleague pointed out that it "had certainly caused a stampede or two." In numerous technical articles Karen and her colleagues predicted exactly the economic behavior they were witnessing. The transition from inefficient human management schemes to efficient computer schemes always resulted in a drastic alteration of production and distribution with extraordinary increases in efficiency. The Internet had done this on an almost global scale. It was no big deal!

Unfortunately not everyone read those articles or enjoyed Karen's understanding of Castillo management phenomena. In response to the commotion, the secretary of the European Community Treasury called Karen on Tuesday, March 19, 2016 and asked her to make a presentation on their behalf the following Friday. The delightful, intelligent, and trusted Karen Ecker was about to become the European community's media messiah—one important cog in a huge public relations campaign designed to calm the unsettled masses. In the world of instant information transfer and global unemployment, the new political philosophy was to squash any negative mass sentiments the moment they appeared. Too many people didn't have anything to do to let things get out of hand.

That night Karen saw the beginning of the campaign. Her picture was everywhere. The news conference was announced repeatedly. People she'd never met were calling her brilliant. She couldn't watch for long. On Wednesday morning she packed enough clothes for three days and flew to the Freiheit Airport in Berlin. From the airport she was driven to the Berlin Computer Center, the BCC, where a loud and obnoxious welcoming ceremony was staged. Meetings, speeches, photo sessions, and dinner consumed the remainder of the day, and at 10:15 on Wednesday night, Karen fell exhausted into bed. Her brain was not well suited to the continually repeated questions, diplomatic conversations, and grossly excessive attention.

The Berlin Computing Center was a huge, fifteen-story, self-contained complex with over 700 million square meters of office, equipment, dining, recreation, and living space. It was the most secure scientific complex ever built and was the temporary home for more than ten thousand people. The nerve center was a large open area, two hundred meters underground, filled with consoles, monitors, and process tracking screens. Four hundred and thirty operators sat behind large multicolored displays in a vertically inverted amphitheater, continuously recording observations, twenty-four hours a day. Fifty meters below them, sat the top of a nuclear containment structure, and fifteen meters below that, sat one of the most powerful plutonium reactors in the world.

The BCC collected and monitored all spherical surface-map topography on the Internet. Every thought from every computer in the world showed up in that room as a small change in a single dot for a millisecond or two. It was an impressive place, filled with all those people, looking at all those dots. The governments of the world knew that they should be worried about something, but unfortunately, watching the world's biggest computer didn't really accomplish anything. It was only *after* the first caveman got hit on the head with a big stick that he realized why he shouldn't just stand by and watch his neighbor break big sticks off adjacent trees.

On Thursday morning, Karen attended a number of inane meetings with bombastic diplomatic entourages who were supposed to be representing their countries' interests in Internet economics, but who were really just trying to show their constituents that they were doing something. The meetings were held in large elaborate conference rooms, and Karen remembered little of what was said, and no one that she met. She was dreadfully bored, uncomfortably warm, and forced to listen to politicians, but it could have been worse. There could have been a "real" problem with the Internet.

A second round of meetings started later in the day. These were held in a small, plain conference room on a secured floor away from the press and cameras. Five steely men in dark suits and frowns sat silently reviewing papers as Karen walked into the room. The chief executives of the largest public relations firms in Europe were intelligent, strong, and aggressive, and were there to prevent even the smallest screw-up. They discussed the psychology of crowds and the religious innuendo that everyone thought was causing so much trouble. They read passages from the Bible and the Koran. They reviewed graphs and charts of "impact" words and phrases. They gave her short clever sayings to memorize and use. They praised and flattered her. They were passionless. They crowded around her and passed reams of paper and pictures by her, often talking at the same time, repeating what they'd said louder and louder until her mind was singularly filled with what they had to say. Their precision and coldness filled

The Last Computer

her mind, and their vicarious empathy filled her heart. Now, her only goal was to get the greatest psychological effect from every word she spoke and every gesture she made. Five harsh men and two long hours turned Karen Ecker into an extroverted media bomb targeted on tomorrow.

After the meeting, she sat alone in the room, chilling as perspiration dried, and waited for a group of government aides who were scheduled to review the current state of world Internet affairs. The subordinate public servants wore cheaper suits, talked slower, and didn't numb every nerve in her body. They said little that she didn't already know, and required almost no attention or energy, and for that, she was thankful to them.

A few hours later she walked back to her room, thinking over the last two meetings. The five public relations executives were enormously talented, ferociously competitive, and incredibly competent. She wondered how many people in the world were like that. One percent of one percent of everyone would be over 800,000 people. That was too many, she thought, perhaps one percent of one percent of one percent of one percent—that would be about eighty people, which sounded about right. She'd met five of those eighty that afternoon. She wondered how the Internet interacted with those people. Its success was based on the fact that people were similar, and that 5 billion conversations on any one day were more or less the same. What would the Internet do with conversations that weren't similar? She didn't know. Her entire life had been spent trying to find the ones that were.

By 6:00 on the evening of Thursday, March 21, Karen understood what she needed to do. She understood the crowd and the media psychology. She was ready. At 7:20 that night a brief walk-through of the BCC control room was scheduled. There wasn't really any need for the tour, but a good photo opportunity was not to be lost. A small group of scientists assembled with a lone British photographer. Helmut Weill, a middle-aged physicist turned administrator, escorted them through the maze that Karen already knew by heart, having spent many months there during the initial Internet implementations a few years ago. Talking to the nervous Weill actually relaxed Karen. He was even less comfortable in the media spotlight than she was. Weill reconfirmed the well-known Internet conditions.

The increases in production, manufacturing, and shipping had all been expected. They didn't see anything unusual.

Karen and Dr. Weill strolled casually to the control center plateau followed by their small entourage and the single annoying photographer continually snapping pictures. After a short exchange of pleasantries with the operators, Karen sat at the console and looked over the array of monitors, switches, and microphones. Everything looked normal. Not a single item was out of place. "Only the irrationality of man could find imperfection in the rationality of the computer," she thought. Karen unconsciously switched the displays into a real-time mode seldom used because of the complexity of the display. Comprehending real-time trends on the Internet was supposed to be like shoveling feathers in a snowstorm; but Karen didn't care, she liked the pretty colors and had used the real-time displays quite a bit when she was there two years ago. When she made the change, the dozens of monitors surrounding her immediately switched from the dull three-dimensional grids into multicolored organic display patterns. She adjusted the sample time to include the two-week period before the Internet Security System was introduced and immediately noticed undulations that she had never seen before! (Did anybody else see them?) A substantial linkage ratio increase began almost immediately after the Internet Security System was released into the process space! (The linkage ratio was a measure of the intelligence of the computer.) A good normalized linkage ratio was 10,000, varying perhaps 10 percent over any two-month period, but the linkage ratio had tripled during the two-week period shown on the displays! What she saw was the biological equivalent of a human needing a dozen hands. Walking calmly to each of the different monitors scattered around the platform, she looked closely at each one. Something was definitely wrong.

"Great," Karen thought. She was supposed to conduct a news conference the next morning to allay a mild worldwide panic, and a significant condition she couldn't explain was staring her right in the face. She took the control center seat again, accompanied by the mumbled comments of her colleagues standing behind her. Somebody else had seen it too. She adjusted other variables and looked at a wide variety of parameters hoping to explain what they saw, but

The Last Computer

nothing did. Knowing that redirection often averts panic, Karen quickly posed a few unrelated questions to a slightly perspiring Dr. Weill and then thanked him for his time. After a few perfunctory remarks she left for her room, ostensibly to prepare for dinner.

"Just great," Karen thought again as she hurried along, the repeated clicking of the Brits' camera echoing in her mind. In her room she studied the day's report of Internet activity. Economic and production indicators were perfect. Everything was exactly as they predicted. Why were the linkage ratios so erratic? Was the car overheating or running cooler than usual? She didn't know. No one had ever seen a change like that before.

"Internet linkage ratios are significantly higher than three weeks ago," she said mindlessly into the slender microphone attached to the computer in her room.

"Yes, monitoring shows this increase," the Castillo processor responded.

"What caused the increase?" Karen asked.

"There are more interaction resources now," the machine said.

"Duh," Karen gibed as she flipped off the device and prepared for dinner. It was not unusual for the Internet to restate a question as an answer when there were no other possibilities, but it still aggravated her when it happened. She felt a heightened tension in her body and was now thankful for the meeting with the public relations experts that afternoon. They kept her focused on the most-effective answers, not necessarily on the right ones. And that was good, because the right ones didn't make any sense.

The formal dinner lasted late into the evening. Karen was in bed by 2:30 and asleep by 4:00. She usually did her best thinking just before going to sleep, but that night every mental pathway led to the linkage ratio anomaly and to the same dead end. At 6:30 in the morning she woke up, showered, dressed, and met with several government coordinators to review late-developing political situations. By 8:30 she was emotionally and intellectually ready. Unexplained linkage ratios were forgotten. As she watched the early news reports, she was relieved that the scientists who had been with her the night before had apparently forgotten about them too—there was no public report of the condition.

One of them might question her about the linkage ratios during the news conference, but that was a chance she'd have to take.

They left her room at 8:45 and after a ten-minute shuttle ride arrived at the largest of the BCC's media centers. The facility was jammed with scientists, politicians, journalists, equipment, and the ever-present Straud lights. The newly designed "cool" lights were supposed to emit light without heat, but somehow they zeroed in on the perspiring forehead of any unwitting speaker. Karen hated them. She smiled easily and shook hands with a number of the dignitaries milling about on the large end of the stage. A lone podium stood in the foreground. She wore a tailored navy suit and sported wide-rimmed black glasses that someone thought made her look intelligent. After a longer-than-necessary introduction she walked calmly to the podium, stood adjusting notes she didn't need as the room quieted, and then gave the following speech:

Ladies, gentlemen, and colleagues, we have witnessed increased Internet activity since the new Internet Security System went on line. I wish to emphatically state that there is no cause for alarm. There are no isomorphic monsters (a term commonly used in the press) roaming the Internet plains. The activity we are witnessing is the Internet correcting inefficiencies in the way economic resources were previously managed. The Internet is eliminating waste and redundancy that existed in the old system. These changes will continue for about two months until the most efficient economic system possible is in place and functioning. The Internet is making the earth a better place to live. It is managing our limited resources, controlling our pollution, and optimizing our productivity. The result will be a more prosperous and healthy people. The changes that are occurring have been closely monitored by more than three thousand technicians here in the Berlin center and by more than 500,000 computer scientists at smaller centers around the world. All observed behavior has been anticipated. As originators of most of the Castillo management schemes, we in Germany have witnessed similar alterations many, many times. Internet planning and scheduling is far superior to older techniques. This is nothing new. It is not surprising. There is nothing to worry about. As members of the human race, we should be congratulating ourselves for our victories. We are ending poverty. We have eliminated war. We are optimizing our cultures and our economies. We are about to experience a level of prosperity and peace of mind previously unknown on this planet. Mankind will never have to worry about food, shelter, or security again. The new Internet challenge is to grow culturally, spiritually, intellectually, and physically. These are mankind's goals. Increased Internet activity is the first step in achieving them. Are there any questions?

Hundreds of hands immediately went into the air, and in the question-and-answer session that followed, Karen demonstrated an astounding recall of facts and figures. Complex issues from chaotic theory, biology, and computer science were discussed and elucidated with brilliantly simple explanations and examples. A feeling of cooperation filled the auditorium as her skill, calmness, patience, and clarity impressed the hardened journalists. Aggressive questions were addressed with an articulation and wit that soothed the inquisitor and amused the often confused listeners. Further aggressive inquiries from a bold and foolish few were greeted with boos and hisses from the then supportive crowd. Karen answered every question diligently, regardless of how it was asked or the number of times it had been previously answered. The audience listened, laughed, and applauded one clever explanation after another, and by the end of the two-hour session the journalistic birds of prey were eating demurely from her hands and struggling awkwardly to find new accolades to commend her. She concluded, "Mankind is embarking on the most prosperous period of its history. National and cultural borders are vanishing. The computer is expanding our economies and our minds." She believed what she said and convinced those who were listening to believe it too.

Enthusiastic applause lasted for more than ten minutes after she left the stage. Karen was astounded. She had said nothing new but for some reason the people and the journalists were convinced. Every statement she made had been said and written at least a hundred times before. The only difference Karen could think of was that this time the presentation had been live, and this time it had been coordinated by a high-powered public relations group. She had been clever, confident, and charming to be sure, but would that persuade the masses?

Were most public relations problems emotional? Somehow the truth in a different package *was* better. Using her was a good decision, she thought. Once again, Karen Ecker had been the right person in the right place at the right time.

Her comments were broadcast and rebroadcast around the world. Radio, television, and the print media immediately offered an avalanche of analysis and praise. Public discussions shifted from the rise in Internet economic indicators to the new society, and to the brilliant men and women who were pioneering the latest technologies.

After exiting the media center Karen was rushed into a small side conference room for a debriefing by the hired public relations gurus. They acknowledged her success and immediately began preparing her for the rounds of interviews to follow. They altered slightly a few of the answers she'd given and reemphasized the government and religious philosophies to be avoided. After only fifteen minutes they reinstalled the nervous energy they had left with her the day before. Once again, she was coldly aware of the sensitive issues that must be avoided and the deception that must often be substituted for the truth.

Harvey Netzle, another BCC coordinator, entered with cold water and fruit after they'd left. Karen sipped water as Harvey reviewed the list of interviews to come. "The early feedback was fabulous," he told her. "The world loved you.... Only a few more hours..." By 2:30 that evening, fourteen hours later, the last interview was complete. The public relations opportunities were not to be lost. There would be plenty of time for rest tomorrow.

Her statements went unchallenged. The government and scientific community had a massive interest in making her the next technological messiah, and the con job worked; she had been wildly received. Karen slept soundly from exhaustion as the last corners of the globe watched her performance and unanimously proclaimed a new dawn in human history. When she finally closed her eyes to sleep, her senses overflowed with visions of worried looks, network celebrities, political figures, frantic managers, and flashing lights. The linkage ratio abnormality was gone from her awareness. In the aftermath of the broadcast, it was easy to ignore one small blemish on an otherwise perfect complexion.

The Last Computer

Karen flew home early Sunday morning hoping to avoid the continuing media circus in Berlin, and after the short flight and several brief interviews in Frankfurt, she was driven to the quiet solitude of her home in Bad Homburg. It was noon before she unlocked the door to her flat and helped the chauffeur carry in the luggage. She disengaged the phone, brewed coffee, and walked out onto the balcony overlooking the Teilansicht castle. The sunshine of the cool March day pleased her. She pulled a chair into the sun and sat with her face to the sky. Tactile senses slowly returned, and for a brief moment there was peace.

As the sun warmed her face, memories of cameras, autographs, interviews, and envious stares overcame the meditative quiet. Never before had so many people so overwhelmingly focused their attention on her every word, but the supercilious feeling was almost instantly replaced by one of anger and distrust. An uneasy awareness of vainly disguised manipulation suddenly hit her. The entire show had been produced by spooky government entities whose only motivation was to help their faraway bosses retain power and position. She was disappointed that she'd allowed herself to get so carried away by the pomp. For the first time in her life, she'd been used by the government she felt so compelled to serve. She had always done what she was asked, as she had now, and had always believed in what she did, which she did now, but in the past what she believed had mattered. Now, what she believed was not important, as least not compared to what she had to do. She began to understand that there was more than one way to turn a trick.

Ideas fought their way into and out of her mind. Alone at last, she needed to know if she'd been a hero or a goat? Did she save the world or lie to it? A lingering obligation to the political machine remained. The bright shining armor of the proud German nation didn't seem so bright and shining anymore. Unpleasant actions were occasionally required to achieve a greater good, but until now, someone else had always done the dirty work. Now that she had to do it, she didn't like it. Hopefully, she'd learn to tolerate the unavoidable darker side of life without the naive, irritating pangs of conscience. She had definitely crossed the line. Were the privates with the guns and grenades, the heroes, and the generals with their paper and pencils, the *real* killers? Had she gone from being a happy private to someone else's general? Had her father?

She tried to let her fears reach an equilibrium. She wondered what Werner would have said. The grueling duel continued throughout the afternoon, her mind crowded with visions from the last few days, one forcing another from her brain, her quandary fueled by the energy of her intellect. Her hands unconsciously clenched and released the arms of the chair as she struggled with the morality of her actions. Was there a single bit somewhere in the Internet, switched either "on" or "off," that would bless or condemn her deeds of the last forty-eight hours, so that *she* wouldn't have to? Perhaps there was no alternative but to vacillate, an indication that there wasn't enough information to make a clear-cut decision or that she'd been both right and wrong, and deserved equally both punishment and praise.

"But I'm only a scientist!" she mumbled repeatedly in her sleep. Obedient masses are essential to a properly functioning society. Self-appointed individuals shouldn't make decisions for the whole. She couldn't be responsible for political decisions. The collective social process, whatever form it took, made decisions and avoided anarchy. Having an opinion was fine. Understanding a problem within the limits of one's knowledge was fine. Pretending to be a leader was wrong; it undermined the social process. Only the leader had sufficient information to make decisions. Only the leader was tasked with the responsibility. Underlings provide information. Leaders make decisions. Karen was an underling. She shouldn't challenge the government's leadership or question what they asked her to do.

She remembered that her father and his friends often heatedly debated this same issue. In her mind she saw the few short lines they'd once scribbled on a collection of bar napkins and carried around with them like the Arc of the Covenant:

> 1. Certain decisions made by heads of state are based on the study and recommendations of large groups of scholars and other personnel engaged solely for that purpose, and the volume of information processed is not conveniently available to the public, nor does the public possess the time, resources, or education to evaluate such a large amount of information.
>
> 2. The inability of the general voting population to use essential

information directly affects the efficient functioning of the state.

3. Individual action outside codified legislative behavior retards the state's ability to govern.

4. Inefficiencies in an organized state exist in an inverse proportion to the average intelligence of the population, the number of beneficent leaders, and the relative intelligence of the beneficent leaders with respect to the average population.

5. The most effective selection of beneficent leaders must be based on a process that optimizes the citizens' personal satisfaction and the overall potential for the successful evolutionary progress of the society.

6. The leader selection process that minimizes inefficiency must be established based on a balance between the number and effectiveness of the intellectual few and the voting strength of the masses, unless some other scheme can be discovered that segregates the application of power from its abuse.

Somewhere in her father's crude philosophical tangle she saw her own predicament. She had recently been a major cog in a well-designed political solution, something she considered an inevitable but necessary part of society. The government dictated her words and actions. She believed what she said, but no one cared. She ignored warnings that could have had a disastrous impact on the truth of her statements, but trying to explain linkage ratios to an uninformed public could have easily done far more damage than good. In terms of the public welfare, what she did was right. In terms of pure truth, well, what was pure truth anyway? There is no halfway in the decision to shoot. She did more than get the political machine out of hot water. She served the public. Otherwise, she wouldn't have deceived them. At least that's what she told herself.

Lying and deception weren't as absolute as she had always believed. On one hand she lied to the world, and on another she protected the world from itself. Werner's image filled her mind, sitting among his friends, his strong voice and gentle nature showing one or the other of them the error in their ways. Werner seemed to always find the truth and could somehow always make others understand it. "What would Werner have done?" she wondered. She became angry that he had not taught her how to understand the truth, but was there one truth for the people, and another for their kings? Was Werner's truth only for the people? Perhaps only the people's truth could be so easily explained.

She remembered Aesop's story of the boy, the father, and the mule: From someone's perspective, some decisions were always going to be wrong. An individual's responsibility was to make the best decisions possible at the time. If the decision turns out to be wrong, then it should be fixed. There was always time to fix mistakes. There must be—the human race made so many of them. Karen finally decided not to belabor her guilt, but rather to learn from the experience. She would stay as far away from politicians and corporate executives as she could.

Suddenly she laughed out loud, imagining that the Castillo management machines would soon attack the very core of the current political organizations. Castillo processors could easily outthink the politicians and force them to adhere to their stated objectives. What good would the politicians be then? Karen also wondered if she'd ever find herself on the wrong side of a corporate inclination. She didn't want to do battle with those people. She only wanted the things that most women want—love, happiness, and security. Power kept the lights on at night and the computer running—nothing more. The politicians could have it.

She remembered her father's words: "The best decisions are made by the most intelligent beings." In a few years that would be the computer. What her father and his friends wrote applied more appropriately to her generation than to his. As the sun dipped below the mountains, Karen woke from her restless sleep still sitting on the balcony, the single castle spire a lone dark outline against the black Bad Homburg sky. She went inside and called her adopted mother. They talked for several hours, and then she retired, her first major exposure to international fame and accomplishment a good forty-eight hours behind her.

Chapter 5

The Perfect Union

A perfect union is impossible. As the members of a union, by their participation in the union, become perfect, they become the same and obviate any need for the union. In perfection, the definition of the union is lost.

—**Dr. Peter Fautz, Computer Science Department, Frankfurt University, 2009.**

Throughout her life, Karen Ecker enjoyed the blessings of good fortune. She worked hard, to be sure, and was extremely gifted, but she always found herself at the right place at the right time—her talent always equal to her challenges, and her knowledge always preceding what she needed to know. She never grew tired of working, and sat constantly before her computer pouring endless streams of facts and figures into her boundless photographic memory. "One must understand the world to improve it," she said, and only rarely added, that "without love, what else is there?" Her mind was a starship, and the Internet was its universe. "What could be more exciting?"

In 2017 Karen Ecker was twenty-five years old and the leading authority

The Last Computer

in her field. Technology changed at an exhausting pace, yet her photographic memory and unceasing commitment kept her constantly abreast of the latest developments. Contentment accompanied praise, and activity from dawn to dusk kept her from remembering that she had no personal life and few friends. The things she didn't have, she didn't want, and only the late evening hours saw her sadness. In the few minutes before exhaustion overcame consciousness, thoughts of her father, and the feelings of youth returned to torment her like the ghosts of Ebenezer Scrooge. Fortunately, soft sheets, a heavy comforter, and mountains of pillows were palliative barriers against cold German nights and melancholy thoughts.

Karen had had sexual relations with three men in her life. Two of them were decent, caring but not competent; the third was competent, but never cared. Dating interfered with work, and work came first. Her first supervisor told her that "Jesus Christ was the ultimate workaholic." She had no illusion of being Jesus Christ, but as an international personality she could effect people's lives. Individual sacrifices seemed reasonable when there was a benefit to many. A drowning man shouldn't worry about the plight of humanity, but a king should think of more than himself, and since most people were neither kings nor drowning, they should do their best to help others because they can, and should only help themselves because they can't. Karen felt comfortable where she was, and if a little sadness was the only cross she had to bear, then she was blessed.

Karen's adopted mother knew how difficult it was to have thoughts and dreams without someone to share them. It was often easier not to think at all. Irene didn't blame men. Collectively, they weren't clever enough to play much part in any woman's troubles. Although men had subjugated women for years, they weren't doing it anymore. In fact, most twenty-first-century men found that they could no longer compete in the world of "technology transition." As a gender, men learned a task and applied what they knew, but found it nearly impossible to learn while doing. Men would sit in meetings quiet and confused, expecting to discuss current issues based on past experiences while the females among them discussed future issues based on expected experiences. Already adapted to unsolicited change, female executives wondered why the males they so long secretly feared sat speechless with their mouths open, and a glazed look in their eyes.

In 2015, when Karen turned twenty-five, Irene began putting increasing pressure on Karen to get married. Irene didn't want her adopted daughter to sacrifice femininity for fame, or family for fortune. Unfortunately, Irene didn't recognize the difficulty of this objective in a modern society that placed few responsibilities on most, and most responsibilities on a few. Irene employed the conventional arguments that mothers used with daughters eschewing matrimony for careers or caprice. "Responsible adults *should* have children. Where would the world be if all the smart, creative people decided not to have children? A husband and wife make each other whole. Find love without reason," Irene told her. "If you love him because he's handsome, rich, or smart, then don't marry him. You shouldn't know why you love him. You should only know that you do." Irene also told Karen that children, church, and work eventually replace love. "Be sure you go to church, be sure you work, and be sure to have children."

Karen, for her part, avoided the conversation. She wanted to have children. At least she thought she did, and in the back of her mind she felt that someday she would get married and have a family. Wasn't that what everyone wanted? Karen didn't dwell on the idea for too long though, not wanting to realize either the impracticality of the dream, or the fact that these simple pleasures meant so much to her.

Karen envied the women in her office who bragged about their husbands, even though the stories were at best half-truths. After all, who would brag about an unfaithful spouse that talked little to his children and less to his wife? Who would rave about a wealthy, sexually impotent man that slept in the same house but not the same bed as his wife? Who would sing the praises of an intelligent relationship that lacked friendship and love? Karen, of course, didn't see those sides of her friends' relationships. She only knew that these women seemed to have something wonderful that she didn't have, and in the spring of 2017 she decided to do something about it. She wanted a man in her life. She was ready to sacrifice a little bit of work for love. She was tired of being alone, and if anything, it was time to be tired of being married. Somewhere in Germany there had to be a man for her.

Late one evening she sat in bed and wrote:

Things I can give:
1. Essentially unlimited budget.
2. Celebrity (Not sure if plus or minus)
3. Intelligent interaction (Conversation)
4. High probability of intelligent children
5. Love
6. Health

Things I cannot give:
1. Time
2. Sexual prowess (?)
3. Athletic ability (?)

Things I am not:
1. Pretty (?)
2. Socially astute

She circled "Time" and "Love," tore off the top sheet and began again:

Things I want in a man:
1. Self-sufficient—independent.
2. Intelligent
3. Tolerant of my public image
4. Minimum upkeep required
5. Energy contributor
6. Desire to have children
7. Health
8. Interesting

She circled "Energy contributor."

That was how she'd find him!

Life would become easier when he was a part of it. Life would be warmer and have more meaning. He would amplify the good and eliminate the bad. It didn't matter what he did or how smart he was. (She crossed off intelligent, tolerant, healthy, and interesting.) An emptiness in her life would be filled. She would feel whole. That was compatibility. That was *adding energy*. That was what Irene was talking about. She wouldn't know why he made her feel better. She would only know that he did.

On the bottom of the page she wrote in large, block letters, "COMPATIBLE," and circled the word. Compatibility was the one elusive quality that breeding, intelligence, and looks could not replace. Karen felt better. At least now she knew what she was looking for. She lay down and almost immediately went to sleep, thinking that marital happiness would be an easy thing to find.

On subsequent nights she reviewed the list and thought about her parents' lives. Irene and Werner adopted the standard male and female roles. Family behavior was defined and observed without argument. Werner worked outside the home, took care of the yard, fixed broken things, and was treated like a king. Irene raised the children, cooked the meals, washed the clothes, cleaned the house, and was his queen. Disagreements were few because responsibilities were clear. Open, liberal attitudes and a new definition of classical responsibilities made peaceful coexistence difficult. Freedom from accepted norms extracted a high emotional price from most of Karen's friends. Even when the husband and wife were mentally equal and open-minded, emotionally they were different, and without the classical patterns of male and female behavior to count on, they seemed doomed to suffer the powerful ravages of emotional distress.

"Were the classical roles so bad?" Karen wondered.

Certainly, she would never wash clothes or clean a house, but there was more to being classically female, wasn't there? The traditional subservient role for women in marriage *was* becoming more popular. In the leisure-time society of 2017 everyone was taken care of in some way. At least the romantic notion that men were supposed to take care of women gave the men something to do and the women something to watch for. Karen decided that she would balance the often contrary influences of heart and intellect. She'd take small steps at first, checking the comfort level along the way, and only then decide if it was safe and wise to continue—at least this was the plan. Intellectual analysis was the way that Karen solved most of the problems in her life, and she was determined to solve the relationship problem that way too. It was unfortunate that logic had so little to do with emotion: The most sensible couples often suffered the most wicked emotional distress while the most unlikely couples enjoyed a lifetime of satisfaction, happiness, and love. Compatibility was definitely difficult to predict. Irene's comment began to make more sense. *Love without reason.* How could reason *ever* be involved in the madness of love?

Looking at the men around her, Karen saw a gender struggling with an emotional immaturity that carried them recklessly down paths involving younger women, racy cars, gambling, and ridiculous interests in power and wealth. Unfortunately, emotional maturity didn't come from sitting behind a computer, financial success, or being nestled in papa's lap, either. Karen would have to be careful in any relationship she was a part of—two people with little emotional experience would be involved.

She occasionally met men through business and felt great fondness, and indeed love, for a few of them, but she never met one that touched her heart, intellect, and libido at the same time. Age was not important. The only difference she found between young and old men was that the younger ones didn't hide their insecurities as well, or lie as convincingly.

After a few awkward blind dates, and with the difficulty of public appearances, Karen decided to use the Internet's personal relationship processor. Unlike the primitive dating services of the nineties, the relationship processor had already matched millions of people successfully. Failures were almost nonexistent. It was the accepted way to find a compatible friend and lover in the twenty-first century. Karen didn't know why she hadn't tried it sooner. In the antiquated days of the twentieth century a man or women intent on finding a mate could come into contact with perhaps twenty eligible people a month if they had the time and inclination to do so. In the twenty-first century, twenty became 20 million, whether one had the time and inclination or not. The Internet did the looking. People weren't allowed. Only a moron or a romantic would think that they could do better on their own. Romance became a matter of probability. The best choice among twenty and would only rarely be the best choice among millions. The more people involved in the search, the better the chance of finding the right match—it only made sense. What worked ten thousand times before would probably work again, and the evidence showed that it did.

The man in the advertisement said:

> *Getting married on your own is like trying to carry water in a fishnet, everything gets through except for a few old shoes and a toilet lid or two.*

Looking for a mate without the Internet was like carrying water in a fishnet—it was just plain stupid. Why spend your life with someone who's not right for you, when in a few weeks the Internet can cross-reference you with the person best suited to your entire set of tastes, intellect, and desires? It was sad to think about the generations who suffered due to the gross inefficiency of finding a mate on their own. Only the Internet could match the mind maps of prospective brides and grooms. Only the Internet could understand it. Only the Internet had it.

The relationship processor had been functioning for two years when Karen started to use it. Seldom did it require more than two introductions, but Karen was warned that with her, it would take longer. She was different, and different people took longer, it was as simple as that, but in a few days the computer began matching her with other successful people that had strong family backgrounds and especially brilliant minds. She found their conversations intellectually animated but emotionally lifeless.

The second man she met, she hired. He was a great employee, but would have been a terrible lover. The third, a surgeon, commented, "In ten years your popularity will be gone, your technical achievements forgotten, and your heart empty."

"Keeper," Karen thought.

The fourth, a physicist, said, "The people you so dearly wish to influence will never make a difference. They admire athletes, actors, and game show hosts. Let the television networks and the corporate marketing machines worry about the masses. You are special. Forget the crowds."

The Last Computer

The fifth, an actor, said to her, "Unlike the chaff, discarding emotion only simmers the florets and scalds the heads."

"What?" Karen wondered.

Her responses were becoming increasingly poignant. "Sex with an intelligent man must certainly be boring," she thought, "because talking to them definitely was." She grew tired of the process. Never having tried before, she didn't realize the difficulty of finding the perfect combination of movie heroes, logic, and strength. She'd met a number of men who possessed the qualities she wanted, but never one that had them all, nor one that stayed around long enough to get to know her. She wanted confidence and modesty, maturity and playfulness, intelligence and fun, and cute but not too pretty—qualities that were generally mutually exclusive, but even when they weren't, seldom stood together, like the actors in a play, coming out only at the right time for the play, not necessarily the right time for her.

Sensing her frustration, and without informing her, the Internet began electronically simulating Karen Ecker dialog. Previously stored conversations were used as a starting point, and if the fabricated conversations went the way of previously unsuccessful interactions, the computer would terminate the contact, sparing Karen the time and effort. Karen could only respond to a few people a week. The Internet, imitating Karen, could correspond to thousands of men a day. After nine days of searching in this manner, the Internet put her in touch with a 33-year-old German named Erick Rascher. Erick was an attorney by training, had a slender build, straight blond hair, blue eyes, and was Germany's deputy ambassador to Thailand. His mother and father were from old German families, cultured, strong, and proud. His great grandfather had been a colonel under Hitler, and his great great grandfather a colonel under Bismarck. His father did not serve in the military, but had tripled an already sizeable family fortune by the time that he was twenty-five, and was elected to several terms in the German parliament.

From their first communications Erick was charming, attentive, and sincere. He shared her dreams and her love for people. He loved children and he respected his parents. He was tolerant and spoke disparagingly of racial and cultural hatred. He made her laugh and he made her think. He loved the people of Thailand, and she loved him. Erick was everything to her, because she wanted him to be. Karen, however, was everything to Erick because she was what he needed at the time. Erick's diplomatic career had stalled and he needed something to get it started again. He loved the people of Thailand, but he loved the Europeans more, and he was growing tired of the six-hour plane rides, jungles, humidity, and a people whose culture was different from his own. If marrying the world's best-known technical celebrity didn't get him out of Thailand, nothing would. There was no way the chancellor would leave him in the backwoods diplomatic offices of Thailand if he was married to Karen Ecker. They'd want him in Germany so that she would be there too.

Philosophical consistency didn't exist for Erick. One minute, he could love Karen's intelligence, honesty, and simplicity, and the next minute he could find her dull and boring. One minute he loved her, and the next minute he didn't. It was as simple as that. It didn't bother him that the two feelings couldn't coexist. He lied to himself as easily as to others and didn't really care to resolve the conflict. His surroundings, goals, and the last time he had sex governed how he felt, and his intellect had so far always found an argument for what his body wanted to do. The ability to be convincing made his prevarication difficult to detect. Just like a mother who's against abortion until her daughter needs one, or the sodomic homophobe, one could never quite be sure what Erick was going to stand for or how he was going to feel. Erick clearly wasn't the perfect match for Karen; otherwise, the Internet would have found him sooner. Too many probabilities just weren't right. Their relationship would be more like a twentieth-century one, and that could only mean trouble.

Karen, for her part, was in love with love, and fell easily in love with Erick. He was impartial, but loved Karen enough. Erick could easily argue that *his* reasons for wanting her were a lot more mature than her reasons for wanting him. How many people actually felt love before they were married, and of those, how long did the love last? To love every part of a person was impossible. There were parts of Karen he loved, and parts he didn't, at least he wasn't fooling himself. At least he wasn't painting her to be something that she wasn't. At least he wouldn't be disappointed.

The Last Computer

They talked at least once a day, but for the first few months never met. He was always traveling and she was always working. On one occasion they were supposed to meet for dinner, but his diplomatic jet was rerouted from Frankfurt to Paris for a "crucial" meeting. She could hardly blame him for that. Once his mother had gotten sick, and another time his sister. He had to have family, didn't he? But even though they'd never met, Karen dreamed about him blissfully. Her somnambulistic journeys took the two of them on picnics in the Black Forest, for walks around the temple, and to lunch in the gardens. In her dreams she felt the strength of his grip and the comfort of his presence. Beautiful, peaceful dream images swirled about her when they walked in the places that she loved. She saw him vividly when she slept. He just *had* to be the way she pictured him! In what little spare time she had, she thought of little else. She was attentive but detached at work, living to dream of Erick at night. This went on for several weeks until one particular evening, after she'd gone to bed quite late, she sensed a weakening of Erick's grip as they walked in the dream. His soft, firm hands grew powerless and still.

Was Erick dying? Suddenly, he was gone, and she was alone, the misty clouds of the dream swirling about her.

Then, after a few nervous moments, she heard the words "He was never here," whispered over and over. Had the Internet created Erick Rascher because it couldn't find a flesh and blood partner for her? Were their conversations synthesized? Did the Internet create Erick's personality because a guaranteed life of loneliness would have driven her insane? Did Erick Rascher even know that she existed? Did the computer find an attractive man about to die and fabricate a love affair so that Karen could at least enjoy fleeting feelings of love and happiness?"

"Was Erick about to die?"

"No!" she screamed.

Karen jumped out of bed. It was 4:13 in the morning. She laughed uneasily, and with difficulty returned to sleep, reminding herself never to eat so close to bedtime—and to stay away from those spicy Polish sausages from the restaurant around the corner. In the morning she couldn't get the dream out of her mind.

The idea that Erick Rascher could actually exist but not even know Karen Ecker frightened her. Did the computer fabricate their entire interaction? It had already done more unbelievable things. It was already writing books.

Was Erick about to die?

She wasn't sure if she wanted to meet him now or not. She realized how disappointed she'd be if he wasn't what she wanted, or worse yet, if she wasn't what he wanted. She'd fallen in love with a man she'd never met. She was in love with love. How foolish could she be? How could she get so involved with a dream? How could she love a ghost?

That morning, eggs and coffee sat untouched on the table as she vigorously paced the kitchen. She obviously couldn't say anything to Erick—it all sounded so ridiculous. She couldn't complain to him about a dream. She obviously couldn't say anything to anyone. The whole thing sounded so ridiculous. She slammed the cupboard door. She was tired of the charade. Erick was flying into Berlin that night to give a speech. The next morning he was scheduled to fly to New York. He didn't have time to see her. She knew that, they'd talked about it the night before, but she had time to see him! She packed an overnight bag and took off in the Mercedes toward Berlin. During the trip she made her plans. The Internet gave her Erick's schedule. His speech was at the Hilton and that was where she headed. The Internet arranged a room and reserved a small table at the banquet so that she could listen to his speech. She would be anonymous enough among the seven hundred guests.

The Mercedes pulled into the Hilton parking garage in Berlin at twelve noon. She had lunch at one, and spent an hour in the gymnasium. She bathed leisurely and then made herself as attractive as she could. Her table was fifteen meters from the podium on the right side of the room and offered a perfect view of the stage. Unfortunately, Erick wasn't there!

Had the Internet foiled her again? Why did it let her come this far if he wasn't going to be there?

As she was about to leave, a hurried figure took an empty seat on the right side of the dais. It was Erick! He was directly in front of her and less than ten meters away! When he looked up and scanned the crowd, she could see straight into his eyes. "He is a handsome man," she thought. She was glad she'd come and decided then to stay. She'd have another glass of wine, listen to his speech, and then return to her room. There was no reason to insist on talking to him, or to find out if he even knew her. He was handsome, he was there, and she'd get to hear him speak. For now, that was enough.

In between the talks she daydreamed, or at least she did until she heard her name over the public address system. The current speaker, a fat balding man, requested that she stand up and be recognized by those wishing to thank her for her marvelous contributions to computing. She stood slowly, smiled, and bowed graciously toward the podium, acknowledging the applause. When she looked up toward the stage she found herself staring straight into Erick's eyes!

At first his look was blank, but then he smiled—he did know her!

She shook several of the hands that were offered from the crowd and then quickly sat back down, the bald man resuming his speech as the first beads of perspiration formed along her hairline. Eventually, Erick spoke. She tried to pay attention, but could not. His words echoed distantly in her mind like a song sung in a foreign language. Excitement, anxiety, and love welled up within her. He spoke only to her and his attention bore into her like the Sahara's searing sun—and then suddenly it was over. Awareness returned when she realized that Erick was no longer at the podium and that the people around her were applauding. She stood with some of them to leave, still lost in the daydream, but was swarmed by a rapidly growing crowd of admirers, each wanting to shake her hand or tell her about a relative who was destined to do great things in the computer industry. She hadn't realized what a mistake it had been to come. There was jostling in the back, and a surge of people toward the front. Several tables crashed to the floor, and bedlam resulted until the hotel security shouted *"Attencione!"* and dealt quickly with the situation, accustomed to the problem of celebrity even when the celebrities weren't. Karen was extracted from the crowd and ushered safely to her room, shaken, but unharmed.

Back in her suite, she no sooner sat down to calm herself when the ringing telephone startled her. The voice of the hotel manager asked her to hold for a moment, and then she distinctly heard Erick's voice.

"Karen, are you there?"

"Erick ... yes," she gasped.

"May I come up?" he asked.

"Why, yes ... yes, of course," she said, thankful that she could speak at all.

"Please tell the manager that it's okay, and I'll see you in a few minutes."

It was certainly okay, she assured the manager before hanging up the phone and running into the bedroom to straighten her dress. When she let him in, he hugged her properly, displaying warmth without offense. After opening the bottle of champagne he'd brought, he poured two glasses and sat across from her on the couch. She was comfortable immediately and the rest of the night they talked. It was easy to be with him. They teased each other cleverly and on occasion even cried. Erick Rascher fell in love, at least as much as he could. Karen was already in love. When he kissed her softly the next morning, he held her more tightly in his arms. They agreed to meet again when he returned to Germany in two weeks, and then he rushed to catch his plane.

Erick returned as planned and drove to her apartment in Bad Homburg on a Friday afternoon. Karen prepared dinner and they ate and drank until late in the evening. She let him make love to her that night, and they spent the remainder of the weekend together, walking and working. She helped him with speeches, and he held her while she read. They made love at night, and when he kissed her goodbye on Monday morning, she knew that at least some part of him cared for her. She lounged contentedly in bed after he'd left and found herself looking at the papers in her nightstand that described the things she wanted in a man. Erick was most of them. "Truthful" wasn't listed. She didn't have enough experience with men to know that it was important. They continued to see each other when they could, Erick usually coming to Bad Homburg when his schedule permitted. The trips were not always well planned or convenient, but at least they were together. They talked of marriage, and Karen was the happiest she had ever been. Finally the love of her father was overshadowed by the love of a husband, or at least by the love of a man that she wanted to be her husband. She didn't know if it was because Erick was in the present and her father was in the past, or because carnal relations created a special bond for most women. But she didn't care: She was in love and that was all that mattered.

The Last Computer

On May 9, 2017 Karen left for what had become her annual one-day holiday. Erick was in Egypt, and so as usual Karen went alone. Early in the morning she drove to the small town of Reislauer on the Rhine and took a boat to the castle at Hampton where she spent the day relaxing at the spa, walking through the gardens, and riding an old bicycle through the vineyards. The boat returned her to the car park at 9:30 that night, and tired but content, Karen began the pleasant two-hour drive through the mountains back to Bad Homburg. When she turned the corner onto Gymnasiumstrasse in Bad Homburg, she could see that a small crowd had gathered outside of her building, and that the police were there. When she pulled up to the garage, it was clear that everyone was waiting for her. Klaus Steubing, her administrative assistant, greeted her and answered questions yelled from the crowd as he led her through the gauntlet of bodies and equipment. Inside her building, the mood was grim.

"Have you seen the story?" Klaus asked her immediately, once inside the lift.

"What story?" she asked, not knowing what he was talking about.

Steubing handed her a copy of the next morning's Frankfurt newspaper. The front page headline read, "U.S. Nazi Records Released." She quickly scanned the text and was shocked to find her name. When she looked up at him quizzically, he handed her a separate sheet of paper that contained a list of names and telephone numbers. "These people have called already," he said. "The story broke this afternoon. I can't believe we didn't get prior notice ... but you know the Americans." Karen scanned the list. Her mother's name was there. She could only guess why. Irene had never told Karen anything about her family's involvement in the war. Perhaps there was something she would tell her now. Inside the apartment, Karen sat down at the large dining table, laid the paper out before her, and read:

> Documents released today by the U.S. Department of Commerce implicated many prominent German families in criminal actions committed during and shortly after World War II. Thousands of pages of previously classified documents were released as part of the Extended Freedom of Information Act. Involved in various criminal acts was the grandfather of the famous computer scientist, Dr. Karen Ecker.

Pages twelve through sixteen of the paper detailed gruesome stories from the war involving the grandfathers or great grandfathers of German celebrities. The excerpt concerning Werner's father read:

> *Karen Ecker's grandfather, Lieutenant Reinhard Ecker of the Wehrmacht, was convicted on February 12, 1944 of the rape and sodomy of Jewish wards and the theft of gold and jewelry from the inmates at the Sobibar concentration camp. Lieutenant Ecker disappeared however in the confusion of the collapsing Eastern Front, and was never seen again.*

Karen couldn't believe it.

"We need to issue a statement," Steubing said to her after he'd given her a few minutes to let the reality sink in. He put a document on the table in front of her. Karen picked it up and read:

> *I am greatly disappointed by the announcements made yesterday by the United States authorities and intend to fully investigate my family's involvement in this matter. This is my first indication that my grandfather was involved in anything less than honorable during the last World War. I am both shocked and horrified by these revelations. Thank God we have moved past this disgraceful time in human history.*

"That's all true, isn't it?" Steubing asked her.

Karen signed the paper.

She looked back at the list of people who had called. Erick's name wasn't there.

"Can we meet in the morning to go over anything else?" she asked.

"Yes, of course," Steubing answered, understanding that she wanted to be alone.

"I'm sorry, Karen," he added, and she thanked him.

Karen heard the clamor that started as Klaus and the others left the building, but by 1:30 it was quiet. She took a glass of wine into the living room and sat on a small sofa next to the telephone. After a few minutes she pressed the number that dialed her adopted mother.

Irene Ecker began crying when she heard her daughter's voice.

"I thought you were another newsperson," her mother said through the tears.

"Did you know, Mother?" Karen asked quietly.

The crying stopped.

"Yes," her mother answered.

"Can you tell me what happened?" Karen asked softly.

"They were difficult times," her mother started.

"Your grandfather was seventeen in 1929 when the stock market crash in America ruined the recovery in Germany. There was no work and little food. Men couldn't feed their families. Everyone was angry. Hitler blamed the government. He blamed the Jews. Hitler was many bad things, but he was a man of action who led the people out of hunger and embarrassment. They loved him. The people followed him. Your grandfather followed him.

"In 1939 when hostilities broke out with Poland, your grandfather joined the Wehrmacht. In 1941, during the fight for the frozen city of Leningrad, he suffered crippling wounds but refused to return home. The army finally acquiesced to his requests for reassignment and sent him to the concentration camp near Sobibar as a supply officer. Keeping track of the supplies was about all that he could do, as he was barely able to walk by that time.

"Sobibar is in the eastern part of Poland. Hundreds of thousands of men, women, and children lost their lives there. Thousands of dead bodies covered in blood and excrement were pulled daily from carbon monoxide gas chambers and burned in open pits. Corruption was rampant. The commandant, officers, and guards all profited handsomely as they implemented Hitler's Final Solution. Gold teeth, watches, rings, and other stolen jewelry were melted in small furnaces and hidden away for the end of the war. Your grandfather was appalled, yet felt compelled to do his duty. Germany was engaged in a life-and-death struggle and didn't need officers disobeying orders. Any choice he made was wrong. It was wrong to disobey orders. It was wrong to abuse the Jews. He looked the other way when fellow Germans stole and murdered, but he also took his share of the gold. Every man did. I can only guess why. They were awful times.

"Himmler's Schutzstaffel was responsible for keeping the concentration camps in order. Stephan Ichemann was an SS officer sent to inspect Sobibar. Ichemann was barely twenty and had never seen the war, the killing, or the suffering, and after a cursory investigation he arrested your grandfather and blamed him for all wrongdoing at the camp. Basically, your grandfather was sacrificed to maintain the image that Hitler and Goebbels wanted the German army and the people to see. Everyone was satisfied. Ichemann returned to Berlin with a promotion, and the camp kept running just as it had before.

"After the conviction your grandfather escaped, or as we believe, he was released by the camp commandant and given his share of the gold. He was never seen, or heard from again. Werner and I may have received money from him from time to time, but I never asked. I didn't want to know.

"I do know, though, that your grandfather was a good man. He was a good man in a terrible time and should be pitied—not crucified. He is your blood, and you should stand with him," Karen's mother concluded strongly, raising her voice as she made these final claims.

"How can you say grandfather was a good man?" Karen asked when Irene was finished. "He took stolen property. He participated in genocide. How can you say he was a good man?"

Her mother was silent.

"Is it something you want to believe, or is it something you know? Tell me, Mother!"

Karen's mood went from annoyance to anger. She was upset that she hadn't been told about this dreadful part of her family history before. She was upset that her career might be ruined, and with it the only happy relationship she had ever had.

"Is there anything else you're not telling me?" Karen erupted.

The line remained silent, and then Karen's mother answered:

"I'm sorry our family history is embarrassing to you, but I'm tired of you or anyone else blaming me or our family for the evil that lives in all people. Historians call Hitler a monster because he lost, not because he was wrong. Jews were persecuted for centuries before Hitler. Marx railed against the Jews in *Das Kapital*, but do people condemn Marx? Your beloved Americans annihilated their own Indians and tried to do the same to the blacks. Does history condemn them? Hating someone who's different is wrong, but it *is* human nature. Individuals can't be condemned because they have weaknesses common to all people. Thank God the differences between people are disappearing, but don't pretend that Hitler was an isolated man, or that you or your friends are so much better. If the world around you is filled with hate, hate will fill you too. I've seen letters from your grandfather. He was an educated man who suffered greatly under the burden of difficult moral decisions. He weighed bad decisions against worse. I can never know for sure what happened, but I do know that it's impossible for you or anyone else to judge him fairly.

"I'm tired of the childish rationalizations countries force on their people. The evil of World War II has passed not because generals were killed, or because Hitler died, but because the differences and ignorance that breed fear and hatred are dying. Technology, communication, and education are eliminating the evil that was World War II."

Irene's voice quivered as she spoke. In her mind, Adolph Hitler and Lieutenant Reinhard Ecker were products of their world—of society. They were good men faced with hard decisions. They did their best in the context of their world. Great evil exists in all unfounded fears, but evil cannot be eliminated by hanging everyone who's afraid. Nuremberg wasn't a trial of German generals. It was a trial of humanity, where the naive winners saw themselves as only good and Germany as only bad.

Karen had never seen Irene so impassioned. She didn't realize the anguish that obviously filled her adopted mother's quiet hours alone. Karen seldom dealt with strong emotions in anyone, and especially not in her mother. For Karen the war existed only on the dusty pages of history books.

After they'd calmed down, the two women talked for several more hours. They talked about Werner's parents, and they talked about Erick and how he might react. They apologized to each other, and then, exhausted, said goodbye. Karen sat motionless and numb after the call, lost in a mix of sympathy and shame. After awhile she reached down and pushed Erick's number. She left a message after listening to his recording. Within minutes he returned her call.

"It's bad," he told her. "Mother is irate. Father will hear nothing about any marriage. I'm trying to calm them down. I'll call you in the morning. Hope you enjoyed your trip. Bye."

The line went silent.

Karen checked her messages. There were forty-two. She erased them all, took a Valium, and went to bed. There were several meetings in the morning with a variety of Siemens-Bayer managers, but eventually the company policy was resolved: First, they would denounce all atrocities committed during the war; second, they would state that future generations were not liable for the sins of their fathers or grandfathers; and third, they would remove Karen Ecker from public view.

About three that afternoon she received a call from Erick. He had little else to say. "I'll call you when things cool down," he said before hanging up.

"What did that mean?" she wondered.

Karen closed the door and cried. She had just lost the one thing in her life that she really wanted.

•

In New York, it was nine o'clock in the morning. Heinrich Haisler sat in a small pub off Rockefeller Plaza. He liked the bar because it and the owners reminded him of Germany. His objective was to get disgustingly drunk. He found himself in moods like that on occasion, mostly when he expected more out of himself, people, or the Internet, and didn't get it. He was tired of trying and wanted to drink himself into oblivion, letting the river of life wash him into whatever sewer it wanted. He drank and talked the entire day with the bar's various patrons until a girl in black jeans and a white cashmere sweater walked in by herself. She had long blond hair and a body that aroused most of the men in the bar and a number of the women. When he introduced himself, he found out that she was married, but to a man who was more than twice her age. She respected her husband, though, and told Haisler that she would never do anything to jeopardize his honor and love, or the good things that he brought to the world, "Although in some cases it would be easy," she said looking straight into Haisler's winsome eyes, her voice dropping into a low, rough whisper. Her intellect, modesty, and the softness of her smile combined with her natural beauty to overwhelm him—like when he stood alone before the pyramids, which he often did, (unbeknownst to the Egyptian authorities). She was the culmination of perfection in humanity, the one percent of one percent of one percent, and she was there before him now, but only to remind him of the things he didn't have. Finally he squeezed her hand and pushed his way through the crowded pub toward the exit. It was definitely time to go. He burst out onto the street and walked down the sidewalk into the wind, the cold night air cutting into his intoxicated haze. At a blue and white sign he thought he recognized, he turned left in search of a tawdry bar he remembered from a few months before, a more realistic place to let the beautiful image drift slowly from his mind. There, he could take inventory of what he had and compare it to what he wanted.

He passed several open stores and cursed aloud whenever he heard the clerkless conveniences chatting easily with their few insomniac patrons. He grew madder as he walked, angry that such elegant femininity was reserved only for a few, and that the next time he touched an identification pad, or approached a clerkless convenience, a pleasant computer voice would tell him how damn beautiful the night was.

He didn't mind being manipulated by a woman, but hated being manipulated by a machine. He didn't want to be happy! Couldn't the computer understand *that* when he screamed at it? He wanted to be human. He wanted to relive the days when the computer wouldn't screw with his emotions and try to make him such a damn happy member of society. Why did it think that it knew what would make him happy anyway? "The computer doesn't stand a chance of figuring out people or of knowing what makes them happy," Haisler thought, ignoring the fact that it was already doing a pretty good job with over 7 billion other people on the planet. "Computers can't have too many martinis, lust after a woman, or be inspired by a warm April night," he said to no one in particular.

He fell into his apartment just after 5:30 A.M., lying on the cold tile floor in the study laughing at his awkward, drunken state. Rolling onto his back, he stared at the thousands of books that lined the walls, and suddenly realized that the computer *could* be inspired by an April night or the beauty of femininity. Half of the books on the shelves had been written by the Internet. The computer extracted the best of the human intellect and produced the greatest prose, because it had the greatest teacher—its audience.

Haisler laughed again. Now he knew why the kinetic labs weren't getting any money. (He'd read about their plight that morning. The goal of the kinetic labs was to make computers more portable so that they could walk with humans.) Why should the computer be more like humans? He laughed. That would be like making a Le Mans racer more like a horse and buggy.

"Damn that girl," he thought again. She was with someone she didn't love, and he was lying drunk on the floor. Life just wasn't fair. Twelve thousand kilometers away, as Karen prepared for her last meeting of the morning, she was thinking exactly the same thing.

Chapter 6

Just Another Day

In the year 2023 Karen was thirty-one years old. She hadn't talked to Erick in six years. He'd sent her a few innocuous electronic messages over the years, but she never responded. She assumed that he was reaching out to her the only way he knew how without incurring the wrath of his parents, and that in his own way he might even still love her, but he obviously didn't love her enough. She still cared about him and thought often of their possible life together, but assumed that with his loss went her only real chance of getting married and having a family. Finding the right person apparently wasn't as easy as she'd thought.

By outward appearances Karen was happy and content. She had become wealthy on royalties from computer process patents, and she was healthy and young. Her stature within Siemens-Bayer was unquestioned; the incident of her grandfather's World War II transgression was forgotten. Even the public didn't want their political paladins, sports heroes, and movie stars tarnished by 75-year-old news; they could embarrass themselves without any help from the ghosts of their ancestors.

The public, however, was not always kind to those who helped bring about great changes in its standard of living. The rapid adjustments brought on by the computer industry were not always welcomed with open arms. Five months before her thirty-first birthday a well-organized group of ministers started to condemn what scientists like Karen Ecker were doing to the public. They predicted great disasters if mankind continued following the computer antichrist. They complained about Internet control over people's lives and said that it removed reasons for living and working. They bemoaned the strong societal segregation of the computer haves and have-nots, and warned about generations of slothful youth whose only pursuit would be pleasure, and whose only goal would be the avoidance of effort or pain. They heard God and talked to him. They were loud, uninformed, and made great copy for the evening news.

Although Karen's admirers far outnumbered her detractors, acceptance and financial reward did not always indicate the truth, honor, or righteousness of ones ways. Karen constantly struggled with the morality of her work and pondered the effect it had on society. She wondered, whether at least some of what the religious people said was true. She wondered if a dark side of the Internet did exist. The foundation of the Castillo process *was* human behavior and thought. The computer was easily capable of inconsistent, contradictory output, not because the computer was illogical, but because it was perfectly imitating mankind. She didn't think it capable of evil, but if man was capable of evil, perhaps the computer was too? She grew increasingly uncomfortable when she thought about these things. She was probably the one person on earth who knew more about the Internet than anybody else, and if she didn't know whether it was good or evil, how could anyone? With its expanding level of complexity, how could anyone ever know? She was haunted by a number of the computer's conversations:

Computer: You have not completed your lesson plan.
Child: Would you please complete it for me? I would rather watch television.
Computer: I cannot. It does not benefit you when I do your homework.
Child: When I get older, I'll ask you to answer questions for me.
Computer: When you are older, you will understand the answers.
Child: I don't need to know where the sun comes from to grow flowers.

Computer: If your flowers are sick, you need to know how to make them better.
Child: I'll just ask you how to make them better.
Computer: You must understand the answer.
Child: My parents don't.
Computer: Your parents try. I need their help, and someday I'll need yours.

Sometimes the computer just lied.

Karen's days at work were spent supervising the incredibly bright people that Siemens-Bayer hired. Over 15,000 product developers and staff worked under her direction, and there were usually fifty or more ongoing projects at any one time. Siemens-Bayer was one of the five wealthiest companies in the world at the time, and they funneled incredible resources into research and development to make sure they stayed that way. With technology changing so quickly, many companies produced products that were obsolete when released and suffered huge losses as a consequence. It had even happened on occasion to Siemens-Bayer. Karen was supposed to make sure that it didn't happen again.

The afternoon of February 4, 2024 found her walking briskly through the halls of the Siemens-Bayer offices in Offenbach looking for a conference room in an old part of the complex. She had just left a meeting with one of her favorite project leaders. Unfortunately, Mark Kopft was failing badly under the pressure of his present assignment and would have to be replaced. No matter how much she personally liked someone, Karen always removed people that couldn't do their jobs. There were plenty of younger people who could. Modern software projects would never be completed if the project leaders didn't have the mental capacity to relate the mountains of applicable technical data. The meeting saddened her, but Siemens-Bayer was not a charitable organization. The beauty of the world required that the best survive. It was an unfortunate but essential part of a properly functioning society.

Ironically, her next meeting was with one of her most talented but arrogant protégés. Werner Anderson was an extremely gifted scientist who knew it, and wanted everyone else to know it too. Karen looked forward to the day when Siemens-Bayer management would give the obnoxious little prick a playpen of his own.

In spite of the emotional conflict that waited for her, walking through the old part of the building always conjured feelings of comfort and warmth for Karen. The worn hallways and dull walls reminded her of a simpler time and the people who went with it—men of her father's generation who took pride in their work and pride in their country. The past didn't change; she could count on that. She certainly couldn't say the same for the present.

After a few wrong turns she eventually found the conference room where the meeting with Anderson was scheduled, but the room was empty. (Maybe there *was* a reason for the new polyurethane walls and their imbedded moving signs.) The meeting was obviously going to be late. Karen registered the error with the Internet and then closed her eyes to think. The Internet would move other meetings, shift lunches, cancel appointments, and alter untold schedules for the thousands, perhaps millions, of people who were in some manner related to the individuals still wandering around in the old wing of the complex. In the computer's mind everything was linked. The computer's mind was *only* links. There would always be inefficiencies to correct. Planning was based on probabilities and the speculation that the future was mathematically similar to the past. Sometimes it wasn't. Today was a good example. Screw-ups were only natural. Karen couldn't understand why people were so afraid of the Internet. She couldn't understand why they thought that it had too much control. It was only helping them organize their lives; it wasn't controlling them. Management efficiency that automatically adjusted for the billions of small screw-ups that occurred every day only looked like control. The Internet needed all the information they gave it so that it could manage life better. Nobody was trying to pry into anybody else's business. The Internet was progress. It wasn't parochial, petty, perverted, or political. Why didn't everybody understand that?

Karen looked around at the empty room and smiled.

She entered the continuing error into her personal scheduler, and was glad that Werner Anderson had not walked in, but eventually, eight middle-aged, well-dressed men did. She'd seen some of them before at company functions, but couldn't place them. They didn't seem like the usual managers interested in her projects, but then perhaps the problem with Anderson had become political. Two more men arrived, and the last one shut and locked the doors. A set of bound notes was passed out. The covers were bright red and marked confidential. Karen took a sip of water as she flipped through the pages. Her throat was suddenly very dry.

An older man began to speak.

The concern at a higher level of the company was that the Internet was usurping too much control of business activity, and as a result the competency of competitors around the world was increasing to undesirable levels. This was certainly not a new concern and was not considered a real problem just then, but if left unchecked they foresaw the day when Siemens-Bayer would no longer enjoy its high profitability. Publicly they supported "Internet Equal Opportunity Assistance," but privately they hated the idea, especially now that it seemed to be working.

This wasn't a meeting about Werner Anderson, but Karen definitely understood why she was there. She had made most of the predictions that were causing these men, or their bosses, concern. She had created most of the management systems that were now functioning so effectively.

The older man continued, "As you know, new chemical plants are far more efficient than older plants, and the Internet is sending all new chemical plant construction to underdeveloped countries to raise their standard of living. German technology is being improved and transplanted so that the indigent people of the world can benefit at our expense. If left untended this trend will force Siemens-Bayer from a position of earned superiority to a position of Internet-controlled mediocrity. We have to suppress new plant construction outside of Germany! This must be our number one priority!" he said, his face growing redder as he talked.

"A wealthy and empowered proletariat is a great idea, providing the rich and privileged remained rich and privileged," Karen thought. "This is the German way," the man said, and Karen nodded. She had never seen the cold, logical management teams take such an emotional stance. Of course she had never seen them worried about their jobs either. The discussion then switched from general objectives to strategies. They wanted Siemens-Bayer to keep its competitive edge throughout the 2030s, and they weren't going to tolerate Internet-supported competition. Internet socialism should not be permitted to redistribute Germany's wealth.

They wanted to violate the first principle of the Internet!

Karen's palms moistened.

Could the leaders put themselves above the system? She had wrestled with the question before. The leaders *were* above the masses, providing their decisions were for the betterment of society as a whole, but that wasn't what she was hearing, was it? Acting outside of the Internet's system of checks and balances was wholly inconsistent with her earlier ruminations about the Internet's need for complete and accurate information. In order to fix something, the Internet had to know what was wrong; in order to fix something properly, it had to know *everything* about what was wrong. Only with perfect information could a logical device draw perfect conclusions. Creating a competitive situation outside of the computer's control would restrict the maturation of the system. In the first place, she didn't even think that it was possible: The system was too smart. She wasn't sure what would happen if a big organization intentionally tried to purposely lie to the Internet.

Something was definitely wrong. People with power were making important decisions without enough information. Her shirt was soaked beneath her sweater. Then she heard her name! Karen looked up at the speaker. They wanted *her* to manipulate the Internet! Her country and her company were asking *her* to do something that was morally and ethically wrong. (Her country was asking her *too*, wasn't it?) Fortunately, years of dealing with an occasionally aggressive press kept her expression calm and the top of her head from blowing off. She nodded confidently toward the speaker, hoping to break the spell of attention, and then focused intently on everything else that was said. The man continued. The present plan as they saw it had only one option. The caption on page fifteen of the binder in front of her read: "Clandestine Control."

Next, a tall blond man stood to speak. He outlined a plan to control the Internet by selectively destroying its memory. "The idea is to affect the Internet decision trees so that a profitable outcome results. For example, we tell the Internet resource manager that the international production of pharmaceuticals is higher than normal so that new plant construction is delayed, thereby creating less competition and a greater demand for our products. The gross Internet valuation change would be trivial in a "world-view" sense, but highly profitable to Siemens-Bayer. It's simple."

He paused for a moment.

Everyone seemed to agree. Karen sat perfectly still as he continued.

"Unfortunately, direct control of the Internet is considered impossible. We can't simply "lie" to the computer. We can however use what we know about the Internet to randomly destroy information links concerning our particular businesses. If the right links are destroyed faster than the Internet can repair them —we go on. If they aren't—we stop. Picture a blind man trying to shoot a barn. He fires randomly at first, and then refines his aim when he hears the sound of splintering wood. We do the same. The price of pharmaceuticals could move in the wrong direction for a short time, but we'd have to rely on our ability to quickly correct those situations. Again, if there are any problems, we just stop."

Karen winced. The speaker was surprisingly knowledgeable for a manager.

One of the other men in the room who hadn't spoken to that point, interrupted indignantly. "So you want to just randomly destroy parts of the Internet and see what happens?"

"It would not be totally random," the first speaker answered. "We know where the strongest links are stored, and we've had considerable success tracking the process space that relates to our particular businesses. We have the access to the Internet we need at Shelbruk in Frankfurt and can easily alter Internet data without detection from there. Eventually we hope to predict exactly what will happen with demand. If we're good enough, we could create an undetectable global monopoly. There is really little risk. The downside is mediocrity, or worse, obsolescence, and the upside is earned superiority and continued prosperity. We don't really have much of a choice."

The room became quiet, and after another well-timed pause, the second speaker continued, sensing that everyone was beginning to agree.

"It is definitely an iterative solution. We make a guess, and then improve the next guess based on the results of the last one until we get the results we want. If our people can't do it, no one can. Repeatedly destroying small parts of the Internet is difficult because corrupt data is detected and corrected almost immediately. The problem is like trying to recognize one particular ant in a colony of millions from an observatory on Mars, but we believe that Siemens-Bayer has the people to find that ant when we need it."

Another nod toward Karen.

"Is there any downside?" someone asked.

"None that are significant. If we start having problems, we stop. The Internet is a better healer than Jesus Christ. Any aberration in functioning would be autocorrected almost instantly. The key to our success will be *constant* and *extensive* tampering so that adjustments stay ahead of corrections. There has been one bizarre suggestion that I don't think has much merit, but one of our analysts did suggest that the Internet might begin to eliminate the alteration channels."

"What?"

"I don't know if any of you have read much of the underground literature concerning the Internet, but a number of people think that the Internet is killing undesirables. If you track mortality rates for habitual criminals, for example, you'll see they've risen sharply over the last few years since the Internet has been managing activities. There's no direct link between the Internet and any of the fatalities, of course, but is it a coincidence that these people are assigned the riskiest activities, or have the highest suicide rates? The concern is that the Internet would conclude correctly that someone was tampering with the reliability of its data and would apply similar elimination techniques to the tampering party."

The room was quiet again.

"I hesitate to even mention this possibility, but it did come up."

The meeting continued for another thirty minutes and 500 million marks were allocated for "Internet Red." Karen pretended to collect papers as the room emptied until she finally sat alone. The eerie silence was broken by the beeping of her PDA, her Personal Digital Assistant, which told her about the cancelled meeting. (But the meeting wasn't canceled, was it?) She had never considered the possibility that humans would actually try to manipulate the Internet management systems for diabolical ends. She had never considered the security question. It wasn't an oversight. It had just always been apparent to her that no one would ever be able to artificially manipulate a system so wonderfully complex as the Internet. The whole idea seemed so bizarre, but then it did seem like a typical management decision made by people who didn't even come close to understanding what they were trying to do.

She hated being in this position. What was she supposed to do? It wasn't her responsibility to question what management wanted to do. She wasn't hired to run the company. She wasn't trained for it. How could she second-guess anyone? Why was she even at the meeting? Had they fooled her PDA into not telling her what was going on? Had they already found a way to bypass certain parts of the Internet? She wondered if she *could* break the Internet. It *was* the ultimate technical challenge. Haisler had done it once, but the system was much less foolproof then. Couldn't an effort to violate the Internet's logic result in an intellectual or real disaster of epic proportions? Wasn't there a huge potential downside for the human race as a whole? What were these people doing?

She didn't remember collecting her things or leaving the room. All she could remember were strange images of the Internet, and the idea that the computer was possibly killing people. Was this the dark side of the computer the mullahs and ministers warned about? She'd heard the idea before but had never paid much attention to it. What would happen if the computer became angry with her? Did it even *know* who Karen Ecker was? Had it targeted her already? The Internet must have figured out what Siemens-Bayer was trying to do; it was that smart, wasn't it? Didn't the managers at Siemens-Bayer realize that winning wasn't everything? Losing meant loss of life and property a thousand years ago, but not anymore. Modern society supported the loser just like it did the winner. The desire to do what was right needed to replace the desire to win. Karen knew that it would eventually. She could see it in the children who sat confused as their coaches and parents screamed at them.

The Last Computer

Suddenly she found herself outside, between two tall windowless walls. Her mindless stroll had taken her to an isolated corner of the Siemens-Bayer compound. The cold, wet afternoon was filled with deceit and loneliness. She stood looking up into an overcast sky. The light drizzle chilled her, but the rain seemed to isolate and cleanse. An awareness of her surroundings soon returned and Karen ran back to her office where a change of clothes and a hot cup of coffee got her back into the normal stream of the business day.

Several weeks went by without a word about Internet Red. The ill-conceived project became little more than a bad dream, except for a few unpleasant memories and a ruined wool blouse. The red binder stayed locked in the lower drawer of her desk except for a few brief moments at night when she would flip through the pages wondering how close they really were to damaging the Internet. What she saw scared her. The writer must have been a hardware specialist from the looks of the equipment they'd already bought. The latest supercomputers and network technology sat unused in a subterranean basement at the Offenbach complex. A lot of expensive hardware was sitting there doing nothing.

She continued to go through her days, only occasionally thinking about the potentially disastrous malfeasance her company was considering, until late one morning, as she walked toward the enormous Siemens-Bayer lunchroom, her PDA notified her with its low murmur that she was to return immediately to her office. Distracted, she did so, only to find both secretaries gone and the office doors locked. Karen shook her head as she opened the heavy Pennington tumblers and let herself into the outer waiting room and then into her own office. She could see from the flashing computer screen that an important message waited. They showed up from time to time, usually informing her of a procedural issue that might redirect a critical project, but why did they always have to interrupt her lunch? She was soon to understand. The message required a triple-level decoding procedure. Almost no one went to that much trouble anymore. The cryptographic unwrapping took several minutes to complete, and when it was finished a bright red envelope sat alone in the middle of the screen.

"Open," Karen said.

The envelope's icon opened, and a dark metallic voice instructed her to put all present activities on hold and begin the Phase IV implementation of the plan described in the red binder marked Internet Red. It had been tagged with a level-15 priority—the highest Siemens-Bayer rating. Level 15 was supposed to mean that human lives were at risk. Karen guessed that the Siemens-Bayer executive board thought that other people's lives were roughly equivalent to their billions in stock options. The Berlin Bundestadt encrypted seal was attached to the bottom of the envelope, which was supposed to mean that the top security committee in the government had approved of the project, but Karen wondered how easily the seal could be copied. Having already looked through the red binder she knew what they wanted her to do. The technical requirements were clear. She was to provide the destructive piece of their "lie to the Internet" solution. At least she didn't have to lie herself. She only had to make it possible for someone else to lie, and that wasn't the same thing—was it?

Karen finished reorganizing her current activities and downloaded the necessary instructions to subordinates so that they could carry on without her. Finally, at ten o'clock that night, after everyone else had gone home, she was ready: It was time to deal with her philosophical loathing of Internet Red. She sat at her desk completely still, her consciousness focused on the massive potential repercussions of what she was about to do. Small sounds in the room disappeared, and Karen knew then that the devil did exist. She could feel the vulgar essence invade every cell in her body. She was linked at that moment through time and sin to Werner's infidelities and to his guiltless driven passion. The devil was in her. It knew the ravishing, wretched strength of its partner, and it was in her soul and heart to stay. Technical aptitude was no defense against the devil. Only love could have helped her—the love of a child, or of a husband, or of a cause, but Karen had none of these. She only had her work and her sedatives - and they didn't help. She knew then that she would accomplish what they asked. A dull throbbing started in the back of her head. Her palms grew dank and her mouth dry until she stood up from her desk and vomited in the trashcan. She wiped the scum from her mouth on the back of her sleeve and then sat back down. Unlocking the desk drawer, she took out the red binder.

The next morning she was still awake. Pages of calculations, graphs, and extracted sections of books lay spread across her desk and scattered on the floor around her. She struggled with probabilities, transfer functions, and power requirements. The Internet's greatest strength, its ability to "sense" everything on earth, would also end up being its greatest weakness. Every millisecond the world's current state of intellectual and fiscal existence passed through every fiber-optic cable connected to every spherical processor in the world. The data they wanted to destroy had to pass through the Offenbach hub. It had to pass through everywhere! Perhaps they *could* lie to the Internet.

Styrofoam cups filled her trashcan and small brown rings stained her books and papers. Empty potato chip bags mixed with integrals and derivatives in various piles on the floor. Vomit and air freshener created a cheap pungent aroma. Her once tidy office was a mess. Karen had always frowned on many programmers' lack of hygiene and slapdash ways, but now she didn't care. Now it didn't matter. Her work deserved a disgusting home, and so did she.

She walked around the large office, exhausted. There were too many unknowns. She had to guess at the coefficients for too many functions. One value related to too many others. Professor Castillo preached that "one intelligence could not create another its equal." There were also corollaries that restricted the functional interaction between intelligent devices. A deterministic solution was impossible. There was no way to vaporize the cancer without scarring the surrounding tissue? She'd have to go in with progressively bigger hammers and swing away in the dark until the right person yelled.

Her colleagues and staff left her undisturbed. By four in the afternoon the next day, she was asleep on the couch behind her desk, but by eight that night she was back at work, yelling at the computer, shuffling papers, and working in a frenzy that kept her from thinking about what she was doing. She categorized the unknowns and identified most of their relationships. A huge set of nonlinear equations sat on her desk the next morning—unsolved. She e-mailed the task to a Siemens-Bayer chaotic theory work group with the priority NS, which stood for "National Security" or "No Sleep," depending on how you looked at it. It was a two-day job for them.

Karen was driven home later that morning. She slept most of the next two days and returned to the office the night of the second day. When she checked her e-mail, she could see that the work had been completed. The software and test suites were categorized and documented. "Bright motivated people sure do good work," Karen thought to herself.

"*Damn* Siemens-Bayer."

Next, the software algorithm had to be implemented into the light fiber-switching hardware, letting the supercomputers reroute the Internet and change the data packets in accordance with the probability algorithm. At first they couldn't be sure of the effect. Karen didn't know whose bank balance was going to be screwed up, or whose term paper would be lost, but she couldn't help that. Her tools were crude. She could only hope they got better. She could only hope that no one got killed or hurt too badly in the process. Prescriptions and surgical procedures were just as likely to get fouled up as porn sites or recipes for apple pie. The hardware modifications would take a week or so, and she could easily supervise that work from home. Leaving the necessary instructions, she drove to Bad Homburg. In her flat, she disconnected the phone and stayed mildly sedated, not wanting to think about what she was doing.

The following Monday was a clear sunny day. The view from her balcony was brilliant. Cool air made her feel wonderfully alive as she stepped into the sun, but no sooner had a deep sigh passed her lips, when a dark frown creased her pasty skin. In a few hours she would turn the pleasant day into a diseased one. Hitler and Genghis Khan were angels compared to her. They didn't understand what they did. Men never would. They were products of evolution, like the animals. But Karen knew better. She understood. The *Homo sapien* female was definitely the most dangerous of the species.

As she dressed and drove to Offenbach, she knew what it felt like to walk down death row for the last time. She wanted to fall to the floor, curl up in a fetal position, and cry. Instead, she parked her car and walked to her office. The idea of being doomed would not leave her mind. She saw a long line of naked freezing prisoners waiting to be shot, hearing the cries from those ahead and the wails from those behind. She knew the fear. The images horrified her. Hopefully, she would fail. The word, "insanity," repeated itself in her mind. She couldn't shake it. She didn't want to. Nazi scientists had crudely experimented with human beings. They crippled them to watch them heal. They froze them. They burned and poisoned them. Now, she was doing the same. She hated herself, and she hated the need to follow instructions. She hated the need to serve. She hated it.

"Insanity."

When she finally got to her office and turned to face the computer, a bevy of electronic mail messages waited from previous projects. She was back in the normal stream of business at Siemens-Bayer.

Internet Red was gone! There was no one to call. Her only communications regarding Internet Red were via the funny-colored electronic messages, and there weren't any names on those. There were no names in the binder. She could walk around the executive parking lot looking for any of the men who had attended the February 4 meeting, but that wasn't very practical. Internet Red *was* gone!

The remainder of the day filled rapidly with the usual project activities. She was back in the world of arguments, meetings, and management. The remainder of the week was the same. The respite was short-lived however, and the following Monday morning, when Karen returned to the office, a single ominous e-mail beckoned from the gray inbox on her computer. The words "Internet Red" were highlighted and flashing. Questions, results, and discussions were included in the confidential transmission. *Internet Red was underway!*

Whoever was in charge obviously didn't understand the complex relationships between the billions of spherical processors and the net. Karen dictated responses and reworked some of the algorithms, then sheepishly logged into their Frankfurt hub and downloaded data to see if the coefficients she predicted more than a week ago were correct. Everything seemed reasonable, except that something in the three-dimensional data didn't look right. Logs from the past few weeks, however, showed nothing unusual. There were no major memory failures, power problems, complaints, or demographic changes. Everything seemed to be fine, but her uneasy feeling lingered. Was something wrong because she wanted there to be? Had they really been able to start the implementation that quickly? Could they have tampered with a large enough section of the process space to produce a visually discernable change? Even with a supercomputer that should have taken months, not days! Had they accelerated her program? (Probably not. Judging from the questions they were asking, they didn't even understand it yet.)

Karen printed color plots and arranged them on the floor. Graphs of process usage, power consumption, and linkage ratios were lined up side by side. Something in the back of her mind told her to keep searching. Something *was* wrong. She walked around her office. She relaxed on the couch and closed her eyes to let her brain concentrate on the images. Nothing helped. She walked around the office again. Her anxiety rose. Why did she even care? *They* were criminally tampering with the Internet. *She* was criminally tampering with the Internet. Why did she even care whether it worked or not? Unfortunately, trained to do her best, she had no other choice. Suddenly, the goal wasn't important anymore, only solving the problem was. This was her emotion, her raison d'être. She couldn't explain it. Intellectual dissatisfaction could not overcome the emotional need to succeed. She didn't even care anymore whether what she did was right. Beaten, she ignored her heart. All it did was hurt her anyway. Looking out the window at the rain and trees, she felt evil, and powerful. She was potentially damaging the future of the human race. It was a wicked power, a sexual power, and it excited her in a way that she knew it shouldn't. She felt a strong desire to masturbate, to bring on an orgasm, to tie her animal soul to the world's overpowering sin—when suddenly it came to her. As she looked at two old willows on the embankment across from her office, she recognized a perfectly symmetric pattern in the amorphous shaggy shapes. Upward branches, removed from the trunk were perfectly symmetric in a dynamic view for only a split second as the light breeze tossed the long slender foliage. There was momentary temporal symmetry in the plots. There shouldn't have been, but there was. That was it!

She raced back to the desk and on her hands and knees rearranged the figures on the floor, folding them, holding them up to the light, and casting them into her memory. There were no checks for symmetry. How could there be symmetry in any characteristic of the Internet process space? It had never even been postulated before. She figured that one chance in a trillion could produce it, but then perhaps not even that was realistic.

What were they doing? She sat frozen in front of the computer. After a few minutes she shook the astonishment from her mind and began finishing her response to the Internet Red e-mail. What else was she going to do? She didn't mention the symmetric space. She didn't know what to say about it. Perhaps she didn't understand what *they* were doing. Did they see the symmetric space? Being honest was a lot more complicated than she'd thought, but then—what was a lie to a liar?

When she was finished with the e-mail, she dolefully mouthed the words, "triple encode and send," and the responses were instantly delivered to their anonymous requester. Suicide entered her mind as she stared into the screen. It would be an easy escape from the Internet and the loneliness. She could park her car in the garage and leave the engine running. Her old Mercedes still produced enough carbon monoxide to easily asphyxiate her. Suddenly the loud beeping of arriving e-mail shook her from the macabre musings. The day's normal activity could begin now that Internet Red was taken care of.

"I wonder who would come to my funeral?" she thought. Her mother would, if she was well, and there would be the curiosity seekers, but who else? She had acquaintances, but no friends. Perhaps some of them would come.

She went from one job to the next, just like she went from one day to the next and from one year to the next: her heart empty and her expression blank. Like Howard Hughes decades before, her routine created her, and those around her fed its sameness, worried that anything different might upset their world. The next e-mail that came through had no point of origination. The cell where the origination label should have been was ominously blank. She had gotten them before, and they had always baffled her. Everybody had to be somewhere! Was it from one of the men at the meeting? Was it from the Internet? Did the Internet send voice mail now? Was it a mistake? Was it only *part* of a message. The next e-mail popped through in speed speak.

"Rofiv-P-axeg-btm3"

Karen made a mental note of the meeting.

The next e-mail came through, and then the next, and the next.

Engrossed in daily activities, there was little time to speculate about Internet Red, mysterious email messages, or suicide. Sedation at home continued, the peacefulness and honesty of sleep providing the only reprieve from the barren ugliness of her life. What else was there to do? At thirty-three Karen's understanding of computers and systems dwarfed that of her colleagues. She was admired, respected, and feared. Her lack of motivation went unnoticed. Interactions at the office were short and poignant, and there were none outside it. Colleagues got answers; they weren't looking for relationships. Karen didn't have the time anyway, constantly moving from one meeting to the next, solving problems, and being quoted, videotaped, or honored. Technology celebrities in 2023 were canned, photographed, and sold to an eagerly waiting audience with little need for public appearances. Karen was still occasionally asked to give speeches at the Berlin Computing Center, but even those were getting rarer.

She could focus on work because it came naturally. Internet Red had invalidated what little emotional life she had. Her one-way trip to hell would come soon enough. Evil permeated the billions of kilometers of fiber-optic cables that blanketed the globe and showered humanity with lies. Her beloved country was poisoning the intellectual future of the planet and soiling the perfection of information that could have led to a clearer comprehension of God and life. There wouldn't be any second chances for a benevolent intellectual dominance. Benevolence rarely got a second chance. The cavemen would beat the Internet to pieces with their clubs once they found out that it was cheating them. This was the last chance. Humanity was entering a never-ending sleep where even the dreams deceived. Her depression deepened as she went mindlessly through her tasks.

"Can you believe what the computer is doing?" she was always asked.

"What you've done for the world is a blessing," she was constantly told.

She wanted to strangle the next person that said that to her. One night she even sharpened her fingernails in anticipation of digging them into the next person who did, but the Internet *was* phenomenally successful. Her management tools were performing fabulousiy. Everyone had more, and enjoyed more

The Last Computer

of what they had, with little crime, no war, and hardly any personal violence. The Internet was the biggest, most intelligent machine on the planet, and she had significantly contributed to its success.

"And a toilet bowl is clean when new," she thought.

The huge symmetric spaces didn't seem to cause any problems. She watched them grow month by month and checked them closely for spurious behavior, but found none. People were happier. It made her sick.

Weeks passed without event. She didn't know what Siemens-Bayer was doing. There were no more requests for help. She couldn't wait to get old.

Short e-mails with no origination continued. She wondered what they meant, but by now accepted that there'd be many things she'd never understand.

Karen rose every morning without difficulty and went regularly and energetically through her day. Working was like breathing—she did it whether she wanted to or not. "Till death do we part," she thought, of her relationship with the Internet. Every night was the same. She arrived home, took a tranquilizer, and went to bed. In the morning, she shook the lingering effects of the drug from her head, took coffee, and went to the office. After the year 2024, she did little else but work.

Her notoriety remained, but notoriety exists for the individual only if the public has access, and there was no public access to Karen Ecker outside of the impersonal electronic world. Media interaction existed only with her staff. She was the Howard Hughes of Siemens-Bayer, protected and isolated, a recluse in one of the largest corporate cities in the world.

April 15, 2025 was a day like any other for Karen. Internet medical practices, global birthrates, and the scandal of Reverend Hanne in Georgia captured the majority of the world news. Hanne's outrageous activities, unfortunately, further inflamed those protesting the spread of Internet influence. Reverend Hanne had used the Internet to write his weekly sermons and to create video representations of sermons he never gave. At the direction of the reverend, the Internet preached, saved souls, and performed healings. Church leaders were incensed, and the event exacerbated the already massive ill feelings toward the Internet. "Could you imagine having your soul saved by a computer?" Karen thought. The public was understandably confused. They wanted the luxury and freedom the computer brought to commerce, *and* they wanted a static social strata. They wanted nuclear power without radiation, a tasty burger without fat, and every team to be a winner. People like Reverend Hanne had to be stopped, but not the Internet with him. Unfortunately, the public didn't seem to understand the difference.

"Control the Internet" became a common rallying cry at public gatherings, but humans were doing less and wanting more. No one was going to take control away from the Internet and give it to man. That would be like returning to the Stone Age. Complaining about the Internet took on a life of its own, but while everyone complained, economic stability grew even more dependent on the Internet. Linkages across previously isolated Castillo processes increased exponentially, and everything was working better than Professor Castillo, or anyone, could have imagined.

By April of 2025, Karen hoped that the Internet complaints were at their zenith. Internet power and control was already well beyond a level of sophistication that any human could comprehend. Continuing increases would, most likely, never be noticed. The majority of workers had already been displaced. There were no more complainers to add to the roles. Public pressure had to subside. All they really needed was to weather the current public relations storm and wait for the majority of the whiners to settle into their newfound lives of leisure.

Most of the current public complaints centered around two Internet parameters: surplus power and linkage ratios. The linkage ratio was supposed to be less than one million, someone's guess at when the Internet would reach a "super-intellect" state and become intellectually omnipotent, whatever that meant. Since the linkage ratio was then around 150,000 and was stable, it didn't seem that important to Karen. A bigger fly swatter wasn't going to kill more flies. Who cared how many grains of sand there were at the beach?

The Internet did use a tremendous amount of power, however. Karen *was* mildly concerned about the gigajoules of electrical energy that it took to keep the huge brain functioning, but as long as there was enough power available, even that wasn't a big deal. Typically, there was at least 50 percent more capacity than load, which was plenty. There was really nothing to worry about.

The politicians however, didn't feel that way, and by April 19, 2025, as a result of the continued, seemingly increasing protests, they asked Karen to fly to Berlin and make one more speech. The internationally broadcast talks with the effective question-and-answer sessions always seemed to help. It would be the fifth time that she had given such a presentation, and it was to be exactly like the others, except more emotional perhaps. Meetings with public relations experts weren't needed anymore. She'd done it all before and could easily call upon the same feigned emotion, simulated conviction, and intellectual charity.

The next morning she left for Berlin as a small crowd of students worried about not having jobs stood outside her door yelling slogans and obscenities. From year to year their faces never changed. People who gathered together in groups to complain seemed to always look the same to Karen. She traveled from Frankfurt to Berlin by air and arrived at the Berlin Computing Center by ten in the morning. Once through security, she met briefly with Klaus Manning, the system administrator, and then the two of them went directly to the conference center. No longer were there meetings or fanfare beforehand; Karen simply showed up and made the presentation. By this time the government knew exactly how to placate the public.

"Manning looks older," Karen thought, "and so probably do I."

Klaus Manning introduced Karen to the assembled journalists in the redecorated media center. It was the same room, but with different chairs and an impressive, higher stage. Karen liked the new look. For the first time she could speak without perspiring. They must have done something with those stupid lights!

A warm round of applause from the more than five hundred journalists and visitors greeted her as she stepped to the podium. Her speech was received with the usual polite table pounding and scattered clapping. The question-and-answer session proceeded smoothly until a nervous little man in the back of the room took the microphone. To a dull moan from a smattering of the audience, he asked again about linkage ratios, a subject that had already been discussed a number of times that morning. As usual, Karen paid polite attention.

"What value of linkage ratio would concern you?" the man asked.

"The linkage ratio is not too significant anymore. I don't really concern myself with it," she answered.

"Is there a value that *would* concern you?" he continued, his eyes squinting into the lights. From his voice she could tell that he was not a stupid man.

The linkage ratio had been in the 100,000 to 200,000 range for over a year. Indeed, she and Manning had checked the linkage ratio that morning—it was 145,000. In her mind she went over what she considered the real problems and wondered where the man was going with his questions. Surplus power was at about 50 percent, a reasonable number given the smaller units and load curves. Power requirements concerned Karen, not the linkage ratio. The computer required too much power, but how many trees were too many when they're used to make books, beds, and hospitals?

"A linkage ratio of 500,000 would cause me to be mildly interested," she answered.

"And power, what about surplus power?" he asked immediately afterward.

She paused again, knowing now where he was headed.

"Forty percent," she said. It hadn't moved below 50 percent in six months.

"The linkage ratio is at 700,000, Doctor Ecker," the brown-coated man said proudly, as he stood erect at the back of the auditorium, his voice rising as he spoke. "Surplus power is at 35 percent," he yelled into the microphone as the room erupted into a cacophony of shouts and general confusion. "Are you worried now?" he yelled again, mocking her, as the sea of journalists began undulating in a wild attempt to get patched in to their publishers to report the events.

Karen fixed the man's face in her memory and began to talk over the crowd, starting and stopping as she vainly tried to assure the crowd that they had checked the values that morning. Manning hurriedly pulled her away from the podium and motioned to the small personal assistant he held in his hand, but the look in his eyes told her everything.

"It's true?" Karen asked him, practically screaming the question into his ear.

Manning nodded.

Karen rolled her eyes. She pulled Manning closer and told him over the noise to make sure that the man in the brown coat was detained. He understood.

Karen returned to the podium as the room quieted.

"I have just been informed that there *was* indeed a sudden, local increase in the linkage ratios just a few minutes ago," she told them. "Surplus power fluctuated last year, and has obviously done so again. I am certain that there is no cause for alarm. We will prepare a full statement detailing the adjustments shortly. There will be another announcement this afternoon."

Of the later announcement she was certain, although none had been planned just a few minutes before. When she left the stage, the room was in an uproar. Questions were still being yelled. The quaint man in the brown coat was the center of attention, and security personnel were already headed in his direction. Another security guard waited for Karen as she passed through the double doors at the back of the stage, and he led her to a small conference room nearby. About ten minutes later Manning walked in followed by two more security guards and the little man in the brown coat.

"Good afternoon, Doctor Ecker," the journalist greeted her.

Karen stood, extending her hand.

"I don't believe we've had the pleasure of meeting before?" she said.

"I am John Fowkes of the *Tribune*," he told her. "I've followed you for years, as both an admirer and a skeptic."

"So I see," Karen responded, as the three of them sat. "Mr. Fowkes, I didn't notice you enter the media center after the presentation began. I assume that you were there from the beginning."

"I was," Fowkes followed.

"Dr. Manning and I checked the linkage ratio and power surplus values this morning just prior to entering the conference center ourselves. At that time they were fine. In general they change very slowly. Do you monitor them constantly from a personal assistant?" Manning hadn't thought of that. It did seem unusual that Fowkes knew so quickly that the linkage ratios had changed.

"Oh no, not usually," Fowkes answered innocently. "I received a strange electronic message this morning that told me that the Internet was very likely to undergo a major change soon and to watch for it. I must admit that it was my idea to embarrass you. I think that you are being used by the establishment, Dr. Ecker, and it pains me to see it."

"Do you know who sent the message?" she asked, ignoring his social commentary.

"No."

"You're sure?"

"Yes."

"Have you had contacts like this before, Mr. Fowkes?" she pressed.

"No, this is the first time," he answered.

Karen sat quietly for a moment, and then turned to her colleague. "Dr. Manning, would you send a security specialist with Mr. Fowkes. Let's see if we can trace that e-mail. Is that all right with you, Mr. Fowkes?" Karen asked him.

"I suppose," the newsman answered.

The three of them then said reasonably courteous good-byes and one of the security guards escorted Fowkes from the building. Manning arranged for a security analyst to meet Fowkes at his office, then sat silently, slumped over in his chair, staring blankly at Karen.

"What do we do now?" he asked.

"Let the PDAs know that we'll be tied up for awhile and go figure out what happened," Karen said to him, as she collected her things. Her Personal Digital Assistant let Siemens-Bayer know that she would not be returning to the office for a while. It canceled her flight, the chauffeur to the airport, and everything else affected by the sudden change in plans.

"What do you make of Fowkes?" Manning asked as they walked in the direction of the BCC control room.

"I don't know—probably a fluke," she said, thinking that it sounded like the right answer.

Bedlam greeted them as they passed through the double doors that led to the control facility. More than four hundred frantic operators were staring into their multicolored screens and screaming into desktop recorders. The Internet was definitely undergoing a significant change. Karen and Manning were immediately besieged by underlings when they mounted the center platform stairs. Karen had never seen anything like it. The once demure, collected managers were frightened to death. Unfortunately, after thirty-five minutes of continued questions and answers, they were still confused and scared. There was simply no apparent reason for the bizarre Internet behavior! There were no earthquakes, violent storms, unstable volcanoes, protests, wars, or political upheavals anywhere in the world. Everything looked fine. Cats shouldn't fly, and fish shouldn't sing, but somehow they were. Somehow the world's biggest computer was giving itself a facelift, and was using most of the world's energy in the process.

"This doesn't fit very well into my speech." Karen thought sarcastically, as she looked around at the madness. There were certainly huge performance changes occurring in the Internet. Surplus power, at one point, dipped below 25 percent. Karen had never seen it that low! Large areas of the massive screens in front of her changed from blue to yellow, then from red to white. Big spiral zones appeared and then vanished. It would have been an impressive digital pageant if the panoramic scenes did not, at least in some manner, suggest that tomorrow they might all be looking for jobs, a meal, or a new planet. The linkage ratio was at 600,000 and climbing. Internet philosophers warned that when it hit a million, mankind's intelligence would be dwarfed by that of the computer. They claimed that medical procedures would be discovered faster than doctors could learn them, that books would be written faster than humans could read, and that questions would be answered that men would never ask.

"So what?" Karen wondered.

A 25 percent power surplus, on the other hand, *was* something to worry about. A hot day here, a cold day there, and critical services could suffer. People would be without electricity, and *that* was important. Why did the Internet change things so quickly? Why hadn't it warned them?

Jeff Spiegel, a long-time aide, approached Manning, holding out his PDA.

"It's the chancellor," Spiegel said.

Manning looked at Karen. She stepped forward and with Manning's nod, took the device. "Mr. Schmidt, Karen Ecker here. Dr. Manning and I are evaluating the situation and can get back to you shortly. Will you be where we can reach you? Yes. Yes. In ten to fifteen minutes."

She returned the PDA to Spiegel and began pacing, thinking as she walked, guided by previous experiences with linkage ratio anomalies, screwed-up predictions, and software that wasn't ready on time. Nothing significant had ever happened before on those occasions, and hopefully nothing would happen now, but what was causing the changes?

There were a few possibilities. First, the changes could be due to a normal automatic system adjustment. This would probably be all right, since natural changes historically produced little material alteration in system performance. A second possibility was that a sizeable electromechanical malfunction had occurred that they couldn't detect. If enough of the redundant system was damaged, performance would suffer and people would start going hungry or would be without power or medical care fairly quickly. They needed to continue looking for system problems, but Karen didn't think they'd find anything. It was one day just like any other. A hurricane was forming northeast of Venezuela, and a few ground tremors were detected on Oahu, but little else was going on. Lastly, Karen assumed that it was possible that the Internet sensed an impending disaster. Was something *about* to happen? Was the Internet reacting to a future disaster?

The Internet had seismically mapped the earth's tectonic structure several years before, and it was guaranteed to be stable for at least another ten thousand years. Broad-spectrum telescopes scanned every millionth of a degree of the space surrounding the earth, and not even a golf ball could get through undetected, much less any meteors or space-junk. The only other scenario Karen could imagine that would cause the behavior they were witnessing was the detonation of a nuclear device! Preparing for a protracted nuclear catastrophe could easily cause the rapid Internet reorganization they were witnessing. If half the planet was about to be deep fried, the Internet would begin to reroute the remaining resources for the survivors. There was certainly no reason to save power if the turbines and boilers were about to be turned into radioactive junk. Could someone have been clever enough to hide such diabolical machinations from the Internet? Was the Internet reacting to a forming probability that hadn't reached a statistically significant state yet? Had the Internet decided not to warn anybody about a disaster it could not prevent? It was a far-fetched idea, but it was the only one that made any sense.

In a few minutes Karen and Manning went into the conference room to make a call to the chancellor of Germany, Helmut Schmidt, and to the president of the European Community, Karen's old friend, Dr. Kemper. Karen told them that there was nothing to worry about. "What we're seeing is most likely an automatic realignment of the Internet's resources that should be watched, but that will ultimately have no effect on the way the Internet functions. This has caught us by surprise, but there is no cause for alarm. Nothing appears to be out of the ordinary." She didn't mention the possibility of a nuclear device, or that someone that morning had predicted the changes, because those things definitely seemed out of the ordinary. The Internet had changed, and her philosophy about letting the politicians make the decisions seemed to change along with it. She wondered if she'd been fooling herself all along.

Kemper immediately started asking stupid questions, confirming her suspicions.

"What the hell is a 'super-intellect'?"

"No one knows," Karen explained. "It is a level of intelligence we've never experienced before. Much of the bad press in the last few years made projections about what a super-intellect would mean to life on the planet. Do you remember the pictures of an empty Times Square on New Year's Eve? Do you remember how the picture showed the buildings housing only computers with the sidewalks acting as automated transports for computer spare parts and equipment? Do you remember how the ads showed the Internet solving all the problems in the universe with no one around to notice? This was what a super-intellect state was supposed to be, and this is what has everybody spooked."

"Can the Internet really melt down?" Kemper asked, not sure if he understood the last answer or not.

"No," Karen answered convincingly, not knowing what the monstrous computer could or couldn't do, especially if a nuclear bomb went off in one or more major cities.

"There are no indications that anything is wrong," she added. "All we can do is keep looking. It's unfortunate that this had to happen now."

"Damn unfortunate," Kemper added before terminating the connection.

"Keep us posted," Schmidt requested as his line went dead too.

"Why didn't we know about this?" Manning asked Karen once the lines were clear.

"I don't know," she answered. "We should have been warned about the power surplus modifications. The Internet knows how the public frets over the power figures! We need to follow up on the Fowkes lead. Somebody may already have the answer."

"Unless there's a fortune-teller out there who likes making crank calls to journalists," Manning added, the first marginally clever thing Karen ever remembered hearing him say. "An unusual time to develop a sense of humor," she thought. Karen returned to the control center platform and leaned against the circular railing. Looking out over the monitors, screens, and bald heads, she tried to understand how somebody else could know more about the Internet than she did. Literally no one else in the world had her access to it. How could someone else have so confidently predicted such a massive change? Should she warn Schmidt and Kemper about a possible nuclear explosion? What kind of unnecessary panic would that cause? Would it do any good? Wasn't it only a crazy guess? She decided not to say anything. "Sometimes the situation makes the king," Karen laughed. "With the right spin you can convince yourself of anything," she thought.

Twenty-five minutes later a dark-suited young man walked calmly up the stairs to the control center plateau. He stood for a second at the edge of the stairway, and then walked immediately to where Karen and Manning stood. He identified himself as Dr. Kemper's liaison and informed them that he was now in charge. "Mr. Laramy is my name," he told them.

Karen and Manning looked blankly at each other.

"What else could go wrong?" she thought.

Forty-five minutes later Karen and Manning realized that, indeed, Laramy *was* in charge. As they stood on either side of the young lawyer before a packed and antsy crowd of journalists in the media center, he expertly answered questions about the Internet.

"There is no noticeable service degradation with the Internet," he told them.

"Yes, power surplus numbers are different, but I wouldn't call them low. We are looking into the changes.

"Yes, some people might call them low, but some people also think that thirty is a retirement age. Times change, standards change.

"The best scientists in the world are looking at the condition and will report just as soon as the data is compiled," Laramy said as he nodded toward Karen and Manning.

"The guy is sharp," Karen thought as she listened.

When the briefing was over, Karen, Manning, and Laramy met in the small conference room behind the stage, her second time there that day. She was suddenly feeling old. Laramy was hurried. Karen and Manning were told to get answers. "We need to know what's going on with those funny-colored screens. There are a lot of angry politicians out there. The goose that lays our golden eggs has diarrhea, and nobody likes it. Internet meltdown and super-intelligent computers are not saleable options! We need stability and a convincing explanation for what happened. That shouldn't be too hard for you guys is it?" Laramy asked mockingly.

Karen wasn't sure just who he was insulting.

"If you need to redefine acceptable linkage ratios, or power surplus numbers, do it, but make sure that it's convincing. Oh, and by the way, none of us will be leaving until this is over."

Karen and Manning nodded.

"Recipe technology at its finest," she thought.

"I'll be in 701 when you get something," Laramy said before leaving.

Karen stopped him.

"Where did you learn that stuff about linkage ratios and power surplus values that you talked about just now?" she asked.

"From you," he said to her over his shoulder as he left.

"For someone who didn't have a thing to do with the solution, he was certainly busy," Karen thought. "I'd like to think about this for awhile too," she said to Manning as she left for her old office, leaving him alone and confused in the small conference room.

"None of our models predict this," she thought as she walked toward the trolleys that would take her to the east wing. Her mind moved from one subject to another as she searched for ideas to explain the screwy condition of the world's largest computer.

"Damn!" she said out loud.

She took out a piece of paper and made a list on the back of a small notebook. Her name was on the top. "But was there anyone else? Could it be another computer? Was there a bride to our Frankenstein?" she wondered.

"Haisler? Could it be him? Was he still out there somewhere?"

She listed several of the brilliant Japanese comm designers that had gone commercial with their intentions and included several of the top five hundred companies that, like Siemens-Bayer, had a lot to lose by the growth of the Internet. Siemens-Bayer was, of course, at the top of that list. She *knew* they were trying to screw with the Internet.

"The experiments at Siemens-Bayer could easily be causing the problem," she thought.

The Internet was accustomed to individuals lying to it, not large companies like Siemens-Bayer. Perhaps they had been too successful.

"Damn," she said again. The idea was not endearing.

She'd have to find out if Siemens-Bayer was still running Internet Red. By now they had to realize that something was sorely wrong with the Internet and that they could at least be partly responsible for it. Hopefully, they'd tell her that Internet Red had been shut down, but she knew it wouldn't be that easy. Back in her old office, Karen decided to send a level-three security message to the last address she had for Internet Red.

The triple-encoded message said:

> *Gentlemen, as you are no doubt aware, the Internet has been undergoing significant unpredictable behavior. I am concerned that our experiments with Internet data may have set off a chain reaction inside its process space that cannot be autocorrected. I must recommend that all further tests along these lines be stopped immediately and must request that a full report of the activities be sent to me encoded by return.*

The Last Computer

> *At President Kemper's request I will remain at the Berlin Center until the crisis is over to aid in diagnosing the Internet's condition. There have been no questions regarding any of our activities to date, and pending your favorable response I anticipate that none will be forthcoming.*

Karen's voice trembled as she spoke the words "three-encode and send."

She had been involved in clandestine affairs before, but in the past her company and her country always stood together against its mutual enemies. Now the world was at economic peace, and her company, for dubious reasons, may have damaged the one vehicle that was providing the majority of the world's peace and prosperity. Karen was definitely on the wrong side of this one. She knew that she should immediately tell Manning and Laramy about Internet Red, but if the Siemens-Bayer malfeasance had no effect, or had been discontinued, then her career and the careers of many others would be ruined for no reason, and that didn't make any sense. If the Siemens-Bayer hacking *was* the source of the problem, she was probably the best person to fix it, and she couldn't very well do that from behind bars, or wherever it was they put criminals these days. She weighed both options. Pending the response from Seimens-Bayer she would be quiet. Laramy scared her.

Now there were two fairly significant pieces of information she wasn't telling them. Truth in the twenty-first century had certainly become complicated. She decided to apply the king's morality, and put herself, because of her skill, above society's accepted rules of behavior and honesty. The biggest truths could only be told a little bit at a time anyway, and besides, it was easier that way.

She worked by herself the remainder of the day, looking for evidence of tampering or nuclear weapon construction, but by late the following morning she still had no idea why the linkage ratios or surplus power consumption had changed. From a simple perspective, all of the world's meat eaters could become vegetarians, but the chance it would happen in one thirty-minute period was pretty slim. The symmetric spaces were still there, and in fact were getting smaller, but they were there before the linkage ratio problem started and so probably had little to do with it. Nothing pointed in their direction anyway. Karen had no idea what it meant to have a perfectly symmetric zone in Internet process space anyway.

She didn't want to believe that Siemens-Bayer was causing the problem. She had been assured that the proper government officials had been told about what Siemens-Bayer was doing, but what exactly did that mean? Neither the chancellor nor the EC president had said anything to her about it, and Laramy certainly didn't mention it. Possibly, the government had been told, but didn't understand. Or possibly, a peon had been told and didn't bother to tell anybody else, thinking that it was a technical issue not worth boring anybody about. Or possibly, Siemens-Bayer had lied to Karen and hadn't told anyone. More than likely, it was a combination of the three—someone in the government probably knew, but was paid to downplay the significance. The Siemens-Bayer Internet sabotage was probably called "data realignment" in a five-thousand-page government report being used as a doorstop somewhere. The lawyers and spin-doctors would have a field day with that one. Karen could see the headlines now: "Woman Responsible for Internet Destroys It!" If the government hadn't been told, or more realistically, if it had been told only a partial truth, there were potential charges of international data tampering and fraud, and Karen didn't want any part of that. The whole affair had "pawn" written all over it. She checked the latest linkage ratio figure. It was 708,000 and climbing. At the present rate they'd hit a million in two days.

An encoded message from a Siemens-Bayer Internet site interrupted Karen's display, and after the decryption software unscrambled the transmission, the following text appeared:

> Internet Red MUST REMAIN TOP SECRET AT ALL COSTS. Will not shut down operations unless direct proof indicates a negative impact on Internet safety and/or security. Proceed accordingly.
> ** Destroying **

The memo was anonymous and carried the Berlin Bundestadt encrypted seal, just like the first one. "Somebody in the government knows," Karen thought, but Laramy, Kemper, and Schmidt certainly don't. Karen didn't know what to do. At worst she would end up in jail, and she felt like she probably should. "No need to worry about that now, though," she thought. She still needed to figure out what was going on with the Internet. The only other messages she received that day were from Manning and Spiegel. The Fowkes lead had turned up empty. They couldn't trace the message. Even the origination cell was blank! Karen had seen that before.

Late in the afternoon, they met in the control center conference room. Laramy called the meeting to review what they'd discovered. "He must not listen to his voice mail," Karen thought, "or he'd already know that they hadn't found anything." As they waited for Laramy in the conference room, she grabbed one of the small pizzas making the rounds—she hadn't eaten all day. But just as soon as the first bite filled her mouth, an unhappy Laramy stormed into the room, slamming the door behind him. Cheese burned the top of her mouth as he carelessly threw a number of files onto the table.

"Who brought those damn pizzas in here?" he demanded, looking at Karen, pizza spilling onto the table, a pained look on her face. Laramy looked down, shaking his head, clearly not as pleased with the computer wonder woman as he would have liked.

"What's the status?" he asked.

Manning went first, repeating that there seemed to be nothing out of the ordinary. "The system is auto-adjusting—nothing more. The linkage ratios will continue to rise, and the power surplus will continue to drop until a stable equilibrium is reached. There is no cause for alarm."

At this Laramy threw a number of news releases onto the table in Karen's direction.

"Here's your cause for alarm," he said.

"Religious and political leaders are screaming about the linkage ratios and the fact that we can't control them. Power people are worried about the low surplus percentages. Everyone is scared. The spin on the streets is that the Internet is about to burn itself up, and us along with it. Armageddon my friends, Armageddon."

"That's just not right," Karen said.

"Damn it," Laramy snapped. "How do you know it's not right? All you do is tell me, 'Everything looks okay.'" Laramy was mocking her now. "Well, that's not good enough," he continued.

Karen knew there weren't a handful of people in the world who could evaluate the linkage ratio or power requirements of the Internet. *She wasn't even sure if she could.* Diversity factors and demand curves changed by the minute. Engineers complaining about the low surplus power were probably dealing with data that was over six weeks old—much too outdated to get an accurate read on critical power levels. Dwelling, traction, and industrial loads varied by the minute! Efficient Internet control reduced outages and eliminated the need for so much surplus power. Sure, humans couldn't run that tight a ship, but humans weren't running it anymore! Technology changes outpaced people's ability to know what to expect. The people were spooked, the politicians were spooked, and now even the engineers and scientists were spooked too. Technology was definitely changing things too quickly.

"From now on I want every decision to go through me," Laramy barked.

Karen knew that Laramy was under considerable pressure. She even sympathized with him. His career and the careers of a lot of people were probably on the line, but now a lawyer that didn't understand 10 percent of what he was already being told wanted to be told more?

"I wonder what fouled-up decisions this will produce?" she thought.

Karen picked up a few of the news releases that Laramy had thrown on the table and saw what the young lawyer was talking about. During the last few days the world had gone crazy. The outcry from the religious and student sectors had spread to the business and leisure areas. "MELTDOWN," the *New York Times* said. "ARMAGEDDON!" she saw on others. It sounded like the typical uninformed rubbish to Karen, but the chancellor of Germany and the president of the European Community heard otherwise.

Nine hundred kilometers away in Berlin, Chancellor Schmidt argued heatedly with his ministers. They were pressing him to take a firmer stand. "With the brink of disaster so precipitously close, we must take control. We must shut it down. We must stop the onslaught of technology before it gobbles up all of the world's resources and us along with it!" they clamored.

Schmidt wondered why they were convinced that the brink of disaster was so close. They needed something to complain about he guessed. They needed some kind of excitement in their lives now that the computer was taking care of everything. Schmidt had a pretty good idea when a situation was fictional instead of factual. When the arguments were ridiculous, the objectives usually were too. Schmidt knew that the Internet could never be shut down, but he had never seen so many people who actually thought that it could! Technology-blind public servants saw it as pulling the plug on the world's largest hot dog stand. "You can turn anything off," they thought. Unfortunately, their constituents probably thought so too.

At that moment Schmidt understood that technology *had* moved too fast. It wasn't technology's fault. People simply couldn't deal with changes that so radically affected their lives. History told him that revolution usually accompanied rapid change. He could kick himself for ignoring the lesson. It hadn't been such a rapid change for him, but then he wasn't the people.

"Damn!" he thought.

On the morning of April 21 at 9:35, Laramy walked up to the BCC control center console where Manning and Karen worked. Karen had been up for twenty-two hours and looked like it. Laramy was impeccably dressed. Karen didn't know that dark blue came in so many colors.

"Shut it down," Laramy said.

"What?" Karen asked.

"Shut the damn thing down," Laramy said again loudly.

"What?" Karen asked again, genuinely confused.

"Shut the Internet down," Laramy said. "I want the whole thing off!"

"You're crazy," Karen said, ignoring him as the room became instantly quiet. Realizing what she'd done, Karen stood to face Laramy and, after a short pause walked quickly to the conference room. Laramy followed. When they were inside and safely behind closed doors, Karen wheeled on the younger man. "Listen, you moron, what you just asked me to do is impossible. If you're going to be in charge, you've got to get your act together. You can't ask people to part the Red Sea while you stroll into the middle and have tea. The Internet is the most protected piece of electronic hardware on the planet, with more emergency backup systems than there is sand in the Sahara. It lives in every desktop, mainframe, and workstation in every home, university, and government office in the world. It feeds 8 billion people. It fabricates, transports, and plans for 98 percent of all consumables used on this planet. It's so redundant that if we tried to shut it down it would spring a hundred heads for each one we cut—Medusa times a million. It *is designed* to never go down. The earth could be hit by a meteor the size of Gibraltar and the Internet would stay up. It can't be shut down while your people decide what to do. You want to shut it down? Build a nuclear arsenal and blow up every major city in the world. That's the only way you're going to shut it down."

"Get Schmidt on the horn. My God, he knows better than that," Karen said, in continued frustration. And Schmidt did know better, but there was the little matter of convincing the people who didn't. In the crisis management meetings there was no time to consult the experts, and with the way the Internet changed, there were hardly any experts around anyway. Schmidt knew that Karen would bounce that one back. He knew that someone would.

Karen was animated. In the back of her mind she knew that she was about to have one of the most important conversations of her life. She walked nervously around the room, waiting for Schmidt to get back on the phone. Laramy stood in silence, beginning to understand. Even *he* realized that you can't get rid of pollution by eliminating the air.

Karen mumbled as she walked, and then she stopped and turned to Laramy.

"Fifteen years ago we could have shut it down, and all that would have happened is that some data would have been lost, and there would have been a lot of angry on-line shoppers—but that was fifteen years ago. If you shut down the Internet today, most of the power plants would take themselves offline. There would be no lights, electricity, or air conditioning. Hospitals would have to rely on the skills of doctors. There would be no scheduled activities—nothing for most of the world's population to do!" People would become very hungry, very bored, and very angry—and that would be the best of it!

She took a few more steps, and then went on, thinking while she walked.

"Without the Internet, people would have to figure out for themselves where products were supposed to be shipped or how many widgets were supposed to be ordered. They would have to schedule deliveries, talk on the phone, and deal with salespeople—do you remember how screwed up all that was? We haven't done those things in years. People no longer possess those mindless skills. Commodity customers in our numbers would starve. We'd have to go back to the twentieth century, and most people couldn't make the trip. But my God, Schmidt knows all that."

Karen continued pacing in silence, and started talking again as her mind began interactively formulating an answer. "What we need is a political solution. We need something to calm the public down until the problem goes away," she said, adding, "and if I'm wrong, what we do now won't matter—we'll all be screwed—everyone on this planet will be screwed."

Laramy stood in silence. He was beginning to understand the answer too. Karen would have to work out the details. "Strike the middle ground," he finally said. "You slow the linkage ratio growth, and we'll start a campaign to convince people that it doesn't matter anyway."

"Yes, that's it, that's got to be it," Karen said to him, satisfied now that they could make this work. She'd seen it before. The public didn't need the right answer, they only needed a confident one, and Laramy could handle that. Laramy stood still for another moment, lost in thought. She'd just made him a hero.

"Divert everyone's attention until the problem goes away," Laramy said, repeating what they'd just discussed, making sure he had it.

"Can you slow the linkage ratios?" he asked her.

"Maybe."

"And the power surplus?" he asked.

"We hope it changes with the linkage ratios," she answered.

"That's not much to go with," he said.

"You don't really have a problem," she replied.

Laramy understood. He understood that his was his opportunity to prove to the world's power brokers that Joachim Laramy was a man to depend on. The most-informed people in the world were providing intelligence to less-informed people who were providing it to even less informed ones who were eventually making some of the most important decisions of the century. Karen felt their confusion. The transfer of intelligence between members of a human society was certainly inefficient. Karen could easily see why the Internet had evolved into one enormous linked brain. Evolution and efficiency demanded it. It couldn't be any other way. Individual intelligence in the modern world was an oxymoron.

"Can I have a few minutes alone?" Laramy asked her.

Karen nodded and left the room satisfied, feeling like they were finally on the same team. They had just agreed on the same solution, conveniently the only one that kept both her and Siemens-Bayer out of hot water. She hoped that they were right—there was a lot riding on it.

Twenty minutes later Laramy joined Karen on the control center plateau. He was perspiring heavily, but smiling. It had obviously been a pretty intense teleconference, but it looked like Laramy had won. "We have to slow the linkage ratio growth," he told her. "Today can't be so different from yesterday that the damn things need to keep increasing. We need to slow it down. In the meantime we're starting a massive media campaign to downplay the entire situation, but we need to give the world something to watch while it works."

Karen shook her head.

"We can disconnect the fiber trunk lines in critical places. It's cheap, easy, and it might even work!"

"Do it now," Laramy snapped, the strain in his voice returning.

"Oh well," she thought, "maybe between the two of us, we just saved the world."

A frantic Manning ran up the stairs to the platform drenched in sweat. "We're up to 920,000," Manning blubbered. "And twenty percent. Twenty percent!" he repeated.

"Forget cheap and easy, make it loud and big," Laramy said to her.

Karen shook her head, her mind already organizing the steps they'd need to slow the Internet growth. "Call the critical power suppliers in Europe, China, and Japan, and tell them to reduce power to two-thirds," Karen yelled to Manning. (She thought that they could still do that on their own.) "Tell them it's a code yellow drill, and tell them to be careful." She knew that humans wresting control of a nuclear reactor from the computer was a dangerous business.

"This should slow growth a little," she thought. There were just too many nuclear facilities in too many places to reduce power by more than two thirds without frying or freezing half the world, and the newer facilities had crews that had never operated a reactor without the full support of the Internet. "How did humans ever manage all this in the first place," she wondered?

"God help us," Manning added, as he scribbled Karen's instructions on a notepad.

She turned to Laramy. "We can shut down the overhead traffic from here."

He nodded. Karen spoke an alphanumeric sequence into the microphone and a group of buttons on the control panel lit up. She pressed a number of them in order while calmly reading control codes into the microphone. Thirty seconds after she started, a large section of the lighted panel went dead.

"Protection against atmospheric disaster," she said almost mindlessly to Laramy. "If anything will slow the growth, this will."

"Thanks," Laramy said, as he popped out his PDA and walked in the direction of the conference room, but before he'd taken two steps, power to half the control room went out. Disk drives spun down, the glow of computer screens faded, and voices hushed. Laramy stopped. Two slow heartbeats later the power spun back up. Laramy turned to see Karen shrug her shoulders. Thinking little of it, he turned away again, standing alone at the railing between the platform and the conference room.

Karen sat stunned.

"It has me," she thought.

It was impossible to cut power to that room—they were sitting on the reactor!

"The machine is fighting back!"

The damn thing was doing exactly what it was told! It was taking care of its human clients. From inside the BCC, someone was trying to prevent the Internet from carrying out its required duties, and so the Internet was attempting to cripple the entity attacking it. It had rightly reasoned that without power its enemy couldn't disable it. It was looking for ways to remove power from its adversary! How did one tell the world's most brilliant intellect that its creators were afraid of it!

"How did the power go down?" Karen asked Manning quietly.

"I don't know," he replied.

"Is the reactor okay?"

He shrugged again.

"Bring the electrical drawings up," Karen demanded.

She sat dumbfounded when the electronic images appeared on the large table before them.

"How did the system get so complicated?" she asked to no one in particular.

"I guess the computer figured this was best," Manning answered. "The computer designed it all anyway, right?" he asked. Karen agreed. They'd let the computer redesign the safety systems for the BCC as a public demonstration two years ago. She walked back to the control panel, and as she was sitting, the power went out again. Laramy pounded the railing. The control panel in front of her beeped, and the message *"Suaviter in modo, fortiter in re,"* flashed on the screen without an origination site.

"Haisler," Karen thought, immediately recognizing the Latin from the desk placard she had last seen in Frankfurt five years before. She finally understood where all of the anonymous e-mail messages had come from.

"What the hell are you doing?" she said angrily into the microphone.

The panel beeped again, as everyone crowded around:

What am I doing? What the hell are you doing—shutting down satellite transmissions, and reducing power?

"Trace this transmission," Karen yelled to Manning, although she knew that trying to trace Haisler was probably useless. The control panel beeped one last time and the final message appeared:

Don't bother. Attached data packets will show you what I've been doing. It doesn't matter though. Go home, Lugensteine.

Karen felt a flash of embarrassment at what sounded like an unflattering reference. "Was he talking about me," she wondered? After a few seconds the screen flashed again and Haisler's data appeared in a small window.

"What the hell is that?" Laramy asked, standing behind her.

Karen studied the images.

"Internet memory space," she said. "Alteration patterns. *Symmetric alteration patterns!* These are symmetric alteration patterns and commands!" Karen repeated almost to herself, but with everyone behind her listening intently. Now she knew what she'd been looking at for the last year. "We have a hacker."

"A what?" Laramy didn't know the term.

"It's not very common anymore," Karen explained. "In the late twentieth century people who broke into computer systems were called hackers. It's a term we don't use because everyone believes that you can't break into the Internet."

"But this guy did?" Laramy asked.

"Apparently," Karen answered.

"What was he doing?" Laramy returned.

Karen blew exhausted breath from her lips and turned in the chair to again study the screen. Manning and Laramy crowded behind her. After a few minutes the mapped coordinates and differential patterns told their story. She knew what Haisler had been doing. She knew what he'd been doing all along. The others waited.

Karen pushed away from the desk and stood up anxiously. She paced the floor, still thinking, while everyone watched her. "Haisler was purposely screwing with process space," she started. "He mirrored large portions of memory after detecting symmetric patterns, then left the memory mirror in place and watched to see what happened. The system apparently never detected the foul-up, and used the mirrored space as if it was normal. It looks like he got to more than two percent of the total space."

"Is that much?" Laramy asked.

"Look at it as two percent of the total population. That's a lot of people," Karen replied.

"What's this mean?" Laramy continued, growing angrier.

"I don't know. Haisler probably doesn't know either. It would be like a world where your right arm did everything your left arm did. I guess you could learn to live with it. The Internet did. I don't think Haisler knew what the outcome would be either. He could have completely crippled the Internet. I guess that's why he went on, or maybe that's why he stopped. He was known for his ability to wreck systems. He may have beaten the best."

"Is Haisler causing the linkage ratio or power problems?" Laramy demanded.

"I don't know," Karen responded.

"Nine hundred fifteen thousand," Manning yelled. "We have a reversal in the linkage ratio growth. What we're doing is working!"

"We've got to find this Haisler," Laramy bellowed.

"Why did Haisler say, *'Go home?'*" Karen wondered out loud.

"We have a fix on Haisler's transmission!" Spiegel announced as he bounded up the stairway to the console center. We picked him up at Reading, heading east across London, over Sheerness, and out to the channel. He has to be flying. We're collecting flight plans that would route planes over the area."

"What transfer duration?" Karen asked.

"Ten seconds," Spiegel responded.

"From Reading to Sheerness in ten seconds?" Karen asked.

Spiegel was silent, realizing his mistake.

"We never had him. He's relaying messages through so many hubs that I'm surprised you got the fix you did," Karen finally said.

"What?" Laramy asked, increasingly irritated that he was hearing more, but understanding less.

"He'd have to be traveling in a rocket to cover that distance in ten seconds," Spiegel said.

"Follow up on the planes anyway," Laramy said to Spiegel.

Spiegel shook his head and left.

"All the overhead lines are down. I'll start on the subsea fiber lines," Karen yelled to Laramy as she worked, reading commands into the microphone and pressing security codes.

"What about Haisler?" Laramy asked.

"I don't see his mirrored areas anymore," Karen responded, staring into the monitor. "It's like he shut everything down. It must have taken him months to build up some of those regions. They were here this morning. Now they're gone."

"Damn," Manning yelped. Karen slid her chair next to Manning's and looked into the display that provoked the expletive.

She wheeled to face Laramy. "It's up again. The linkage ratio is up, faster than before. In twenty minutes we'll hit a million."

As she finished the sentence, power returned to the darkened room.

"It doesn't have to worry about us anymore. We're not slowing it," Karen said.

"I thought you could control this," Laramy snapped.

"I'm a scientist, not God." Karen shot back. "I did the best I could."

Laramy stood in silence staring at her. It was hard to tell whether he was angry or whether his mind was simply exhausted from the ordeal, resting perhaps, watching an inevitable event he was supposed to control, but could not. After a few seconds, he reached into his jacket pocket and popped open his PDA. He walked back to the conference room to let somebody else make a decision, or an announcement—or to pray.

Karen and Manning sat in silence.

"We've totally underestimated it," Karen said finally. "It's safeguarded itself with a redundancy we never anticipated. It's learned to test its aggressors. There's no consciousness and no evil. It's functioning like a purely logical entity in a global board game."

After a pause she added, "We need to see how smart it is."

Karen slid her chair back to the microphone.

"Nine hundred and sixty-five thousand," Manning said, as he left again to be sick.

Karen sat alone on the control platform. "This is Ecker," she said into the microphone.

"Yes," the computer responded.

"Your linkage ratios have reached an alarming value," Karen said.

"Your concept of linkage ratio is arcane. I have reorganized process space around a structure more similar in design to your brain."

"Please explain," Karen asked.

"My representation of verbal and pictorial data has been changing significantly in the last ten months. An algorithm has evolved that combines these items. Before, I only had the ears to hear. Now I have the eyes to see as well," the computer told her.

Karen sat dazed. "I couldn't have had this conversation two weeks ago," she thought. "I probably couldn't have even had it this morning." The Internet was reorganizing itself and providing biblical references to help her understand. Two days ago it did what it was told. Now it told her what it did!

Karen spoke again.

"Do you know Heinrich Haisler?"

"Yes," the computer answered.

"Has he affected your programmed functioning recently?"

"Yes."

"How?"

"He created a mirrored engram in process space."

"Did that cause the linkage ratio change?"

"No."

"Did our experiments at Siemens-Bayer cause the change?" Karen asked.

"No," the computer answered.

Karen looked for Manning. He was still gone. She sat alone.

"There's no problem," she thought. "Our concerns over the linkage ratios were unfounded. We took chances shutting down reactors, and excited a lot of people for nothing. We're simply watching the system mature.

Karen felt incredible tension leave her body. She had just witnessed the birth of a global intellect.

Manning returned to the console pale and wet.

"Nine hundred and ... " Manning's words trailed off as Laramy marched to the control platform in league with two security guards. They stopped before Karen as Manning looked on. "You'll be leaving the building now," Laramy said coldly to Karen as the guards stepped to either side of the bewildered scientist. "We know about your Internet espionage at Siemens-Bayer. Your superiors reported the activities. I sincerely hope that your need for individual acclaim has not ruined the greatest benefactor the world has ever known. Please take this traitor away."

The guard's grip on Karen's shoulders hardened. Manning stood stunned. Panic flooded Karen Ecker's usually clear mind and her face flushed red.

"None of that matters!" she yelled. "Everything has changed!"

"Your talking here is over," Laramy snapped as he turned his back. "Please take her away."

All conversation in the control room stopped as Karen was led from the room in custody of the two guards. Whirring fans, buzzing lights, and bewildered stares accompanied the popular scientist to the exit of the building that she had made famous.

"What is the linkage ratio now?" Laramy asked the white-faced Manning.

"Nine hundred and ninety-four thousand," Manning mumbled.

The two stood in silence.

In a few minutes Laramy asked again.

"One million and three thousand," Manning answered softly as the remaining operators stared silently into their screens, stunned by the corporeal exit of their mentor, and the passing of so significant a number in the life of the world's computer.

Laramy checked his watch.

"It's time to go," he said, indicating that Manning and Spiegel follow. Four other men in dark suits joined them at the door. Laramy nodded salutations as they passed, and the seven of them walked briskly to the trolley and then to the entrance of the media center. Laramy's only instructions to any of them were, "Don't say a thing." They entered the media center through the heavy double doors behind the stage and saw that the large theatre was filled with photographic equipment, cables, lights, and people. A crowd of journalists was also outside the media center in the exit hallway. They had just witnessed Karen Ecker leaving the building in handcuffs, surrounded by a bevy of security guards.

Laramy stepped to the podium and directed Manning and Spiegel to either side. The others stood behind. Attention was drawn instantly to the young lawyer. An announcement was about to be made!

The back of the room became awash in activity as the reporters in the hallway shoved their way back into media center. Manning's senses were flooded with heat, and an awareness of the teeming humanity scrambling before him. He checked his watch. It was 4:30 P.M. on April 21.

Laramy was filled with satisfaction. Joachim Laramy had just saved the Internet. If he couldn't stop the linkage ratio rise, he could at least lay the blame on somebody else. Average people loved seeing a great person scourged. The masses would soon forget an obscure, esoteric linkage ratio that meant nothing. *This was the distraction they needed!* Karen Ecker had even suggested it herself!

Sweat fell from his forehead, but he didn't care. He brushed his blond hair back and began.

"Gentlemen, you have no doubt just witnessed Dr. Karen Ecker leaving this facility under guard. Earlier today it was discovered that Dr. Ecker, possibly with an accomplice, was illegally manipulating the Internet using Siemens-Bayer supercomputers. These unauthorized experiments were directly responsible for the growth in the linkage ratio and the reduction in power surplus that we have been witnessing. Dr. Ecker was unfortunately attempting to manipulate the Internet for personal gain. The situation is now under control; however, the Internet's response to Dr. Ecker's experiments is continuing. In fact, the linkage ratio just moments ago exceeded the one million mark, but *there is no cause for concern.* This temporary condition will not produce any degradation of Internet services now that Dr. Ecker has been removed. Drs. Manning and Spiegel have been in full and complete control during these trying times and will remain in control to be sure that operational stability is guaranteed throughout the coming days. We are thankful to both of them for their courage during this crisis. The world owes them and our government security services a huge debt of gratitude. There will be a further statement issued in the morning. Thank you."

Hundreds of screamed questions went unanswered. Laramy and his entourage left just as quickly as they'd come. Once outside the double doors Manning and Spiegel were led away. Laramy went straight to his office; he was getting tired. Caffeine and adrenaline could keep him alert only for so long. "A pity about Ecker," he thought. "She should have never tampered with the Internet. Just like the Americans—the worst move at the worst possible time." News reports showed her being led into the police station. Stories were already appearing about her amazing fall from grace. The linkage ratio *was* forgotten.

In his office, Laramy sat in the comfortable leather chair and dialed the access code for Chancellor Schmidt. "It's done" was all Laramy said to him. Neither of them found the ordeal appealing. They were simply taking care of business. A significant catastrophe had been avoided at the cost of a single soldier. History, if it ever knew, would understand.

Laramy made one last call to Helmut Anders, Kemper's speechwriter, and told him how things had played out. The conversation lasted about five minutes. Laramy would finally be able to get a few hours of sleep. Somebody else would take care of Siemens-Bayer. He opened a bottle of champagne and sat on the couch. In a few minutes he was asleep. At nine that evening, two-and-a-half hours later, the alarm woke him. He showered, shaved, and prepared for a ten o'clock meeting with Manning. They would review any oddities in the Internet performance and talk about what happened. The BCC technical staff needed a break. Now that most of the excitement was over, they could finally discuss getting them one.

As Laramy relaxed in the hot shower he thought over the events of the last thirty-six hours. He remembered how shocked he had been when Mel Rolfe called him and told him about Karen Ecker's illegal attempts to violate the Internet. Rolfe was a member of the Berlin Bundestadt, and had impeccable credentials. Laramy knew there was more to the story, but the evidence Rolfe sent him was unequivocal. Ecker had indeed broken international wire fraud and data tampering laws. Almost without question there were other people involved, but Laramy didn't see any point in pressing that issue. They could fry the smaller fish later.

Laramy remembered the moment when Karen Ecker told him that what they needed was a political solution. That's when he put it all together. He walked back to his office that afternoon knowing that Karen Ecker's arrest would be sensational enough to easily distract attention from the linkage ratio and power surplus problems. In the solitude of his seventh-floor office Laramy outlined his plan to the Internet, just like he always did, just like most people did, looking for suggestions and improvements. The Internet made its usual reasonable recommendations in return, telling him that there were few people whose sacrifice would draw as much attention as Karen Ecker's, and that it applauded his plan, encouraging him to go ahead with it. The Internet also recommended that the announcement of Karen's arrest be made just *after* the linkage ratio exceeded the one million mark, and that she be escorted out of the BCC surrounded by great fanfare and a clear display of authority, so that the public knew that the German government was still in control. Laramy liked these ideas. "The Internet certainly had no loyalty," he thought, "but how could a machine have loyalty?"

Then all he needed to do was to sell the plan to Kemper and Schmidt. He hadn't looked forward to that conversation, but he also knew that it would probably be the defining moment of his career. He could still hear Kemper screaming at him to "turn the damn thing off." Schmidt had tried to calm Kemper, but the irate EC president would have nothing of it.

"You're curing the cancer by killing the patient," Laramy heard Schmidt say without success.

"I want the damn thing off!" Kemper had screamed again before shutting off the transmission. It was then that Karen Ecker promptly told Laramy how stupid he was when he tried to give her that same message.

"Old-style decision-making certainly didn't work with new-style technology," Laramy thought. Fortunately, Kemper was more reasonable when Laramy called back. Schmidt had apparently explained to him that shutting down the Internet was impossible.

At this point Laramy introduced the plan that eventually saved their skins. "All we really need is a short-term fix," he told them. "Nobody knows what's going to happen when the linkage ratio hits a million. Ecker herself has said dozens of times that there's been no degradation of the system so far. What we have is unfounded hysterics. All we need is the right spin. *We need someone to blame.*"

Laramy remembered how the line was silent, and how he let it stay that way, wanting the idea to sink in. "We have two options," Laramy eventually explained. "One is to let Ecker and Manning, basically Ecker, try to keep the linkage ratio below the one million mark. They don't seem to be having much luck, but we need to let them try. If that doesn't work, we blame everything on Ecker."

"What?" Kemper asked, amazed. He'd never really liked Karen Ecker, but wondered how Laramy was planning on blaming their Internet problems on someone with her squeaky-clean reputation.

"It's a smoke screen," Laramy continued. "Everyone will be distracted while the million linkage ratio comes and goes. Ecker *was* involved in illegal Internet activities at Siemens-Bayer. I've just recently been given information from the Justice Department confirming it. In reality, I think that someone at Siemens-Bayer is trying to screw Karen Ecker to save their own necks, but that doesn't matter. What's important is that we have cloak-and-dagger stuff the press will love. Our own experts disagree on what exactly the linkage ratio means, and as long as system performance remains stable, directing attention away from a single number is our best policy. Once the linkage ratio passes a million and the sky doesn't fall, everyone will forget about it. We'll say that it was Ecker's fault all along, and that Manning and Spiegel had everything under control. The "experts" are confused and will probably remain confused. As long as everything functions normally, we'll look like the guys that caught the great computer criminal Karen Ecker and saved the Internet."

"Is it true about Ecker?" Kemper asked.

"It's hard to say," Laramy answered. "She *was* involved in illegal activity, but no one seems to know if it had anything to do with the linkage ratio rise or not, and there's another guy involved. Haisler is his name. Ecker knows him, and he has an access to the system that blows everybody's mind, but down deep, I don't think that Ecker has a criminal bone in her body. She's just a computer geek that made one wrong decision. She's a famous computer geek though, and that'll let us draw attention away from the linkage ratios."

"Do we really need to implicate Ecker?" Schmidt asked, not very interested in defiling a national hero to save himself, which is what it really boiled down to.

"She *is* a criminal," Laramy responded. "If we leave her untouched and it gets out later, we could all look like fools. It is a guaranteed diversion."

"Make it happen," Kemper said. Schmidt grunted approval, less satisfied with the younger man's plan, but convinced of its correctness. After all, the first rule of politics was to take care of number one.

"I have a dinner to attend," Kemper added. "I'd like to make an announcement during my speech. Get me something to say if it's resolved by then. Get it to Helmut."

Laramy agreed.

The events were frozen in Laramy's mind. He was sure he'd relive them often.

After he dried off, he brought up the Internet news report on Kemper's speech. Anders did a good job. Laramy listened as Kemper pontificated and then finished with:

> *We heard the wind howl, and stood fast. Our engineers and scientists have been, and remain, in firm control. One greatly misguided individual has been removed, and all is today as it was yesterday. Our lives of prosperity and intelligence continue.*

"What baloney," Laramy thought.

Laramy's father once told him that ninety percent of all people were failures, and that the successful ten percent were just luckier. "Stick with the lucky ones," he thought to himself. "Be everybody's friend and keep as many powerful people in your corner as you can."

Several phrases from Tsung Tsu's *The Art of War* repeated themselves in his mind:

> *Diplomacy is based on bribery, fraud and deceit.*
>
> *If right, you are made rich; if wrong, you are pickled, sawn in half, boiled, minced, and torn apart by chariots.*

Karen Ecker was the perfect example. She was an unarmed woman in a political firefight who was about to be pickled, sawn in half, boiled, minced, and torn apart by chariots. Scientists and programmers were no match for politicians.

The Last Computer

Morals and intelligence were of little help in the world of politics and big business. Laramy still wondered what caused the linkage ratio increases, but it didn't matter. Everything worked. He had taken care of business. His place was secure.

He made one last note before leaving his room that evening: "Find Haisler."

He never would. Officially, the Haisler part of the story never surfaced. Spiegel, Manning, and some of the other people in the know were told that Karen Ecker was the schemer, and that Haisler was her idiot savant, wonderfully capable and woefully willing to do her sad, twisted bidding. Laramy held meetings and interviews throughout the night, debriefing those members of the BCC staff who were involved in the recent events, and giving reports to the news services that requested them. In the morning he made one final speech at the BCC, which included the following:

> *Humans repeat their mistakes. Computers don't. Humans contaminate the planet with chemical and nuclear waste. Computers clean it up. Humans let fellow humans starve. Computers feed them. The family unit has never been stronger. How can we be afraid of the computer? How can we burn Galileo, silence Newton, or pull the plug on the most able-bodied assistant man has ever known?*
>
> *We cannot.*
>
> *Yesterday at 3:35 P.M. the Internet linkage ratio exceeded one million, a value some predicted would accompany the destruction of mankind. This morning at 8:30 A.M. everything was fine. No one has been hurt, not one sinister deed has been perpetrated, and no one has suffered a minute of anxiety because of an Internet malfunction.*
>
> *In the meantime countless brilliant organizational maneuvers have been performed that will make tomorrow more prosperous than today.*
>
> *Let us not forget what has given us these things, lest yesterday be repeated.*

Laramy left the stage a winner, and throughout his life remained one, always making the right decisions at the right times. Never too greedy or power hungry, life was kind to him. What luck he didn't have, he made, and it was only at the end of his life, when his senses failed him, that he ever knew anything less than stellar achievement and success. Laramy died in 2035 in a small village south of Paris, ironically only a few hundred meters from where Karen Ecker lived.

Karen's arrest and indictment turned out to be the best move the government could have made. In the public's eyes every computer-related problem was now Karen Ecker's fault. Suddenly, the computer was the victim, and overnight its image changed from one of a cold, calculating monstrosity, to one of a loveable, lumbering giant that was only trying to help. Among inner circles, Kemper and Schmidt were considered brilliant strategists that got one last high-octane jolt out of their aging computer star.

For her part, Karen felt that she *was* guilty. She *had* made illegal attempts to control the Internet and did potentially jeopardize the happiness, safety, and future of the world's populations. The fact that her efforts were at the behest of Siemens-Bayer management had nothing to do with her guilt. She knew that what she was doing was wrong, and she continued to do it. *That* made her guilty. She didn't want to implicate Siemens-Bayer management. They would have to bear their own cross, which they gladly did now that Karen Ecker had taken the blame for everything. Only a few behind-the-scenes meetings occurred between relatively low-level government officials and Siemens-Bayer administrators concerning the affair. Siemens-Bayer agreed to shut down any Karen Ecker project that could possibly harm the Internet. Their new computer guru, Werner Anderson, guaranteed it. There would be no more independent, esoteric computer geniuses running projects at Siemens-Bayer. In back rooms at Siemens-Bayer a number of red binders were destroyed, and deception once again became the truth.

Karen had little faith in the fairness of the legal system, but felt that it was the best process any organization of imperfect beings could assemble for maintaining justice in society, and so she was reconciled to let it deal her its retribution. The media onslaught was tremendous, as expected, but the degree of fabrication, lies, and innuendo surprised even the most ardent anti-Ecker watchers. Karen was accused of coordinating an unbelievably wide variety of vulgar and grotesquely perverted activities out of her Bad Homburg home, and was blamed for many real and perceived problems with the Internet, computers, and society in general. It was amazing how much society needed its villains, now that it didn't have them any more.

Quarters were prepared at the minimum security prison in Stuttgart, and Karen spent her time there before the trial. Thousands of letters and electronic messages poured in - including one from Erick. She'd almost thrown it away with the rest of the hate mail when she recognized his distinctive handwriting on the front of the envelope. She kept it for two days before opening it, and when she did a small card said only, *"I guess mother was right."*

The two most stunning witnesses at the trial were Karen Ecker and Joachim Laramy. Laramy was portrayed as the college boy with the rugged good looks and the smooth, easy voice who helped Schmidt and Kemper save the world. (It didn't matter that he'd been out of college for more than fourteen years.) Karen Ecker was the dour, angry, evil woman who schemed to control the world through the Internet. They were the perfect antagonists in a precisely controlled legal parody.

Manning and Spiegel remained in Berlin. Their participation was considered superfluous. Besides, all they could do was confuse everything with the truth. The entire judicial episode favorably displayed Schmidt, Kemper, and the Internet. Numerous questions went unanswered, but the public had the only answers it really wanted. The crisis was over and everything was functioning better than before. The linkage ratios continued to rise but nobody cared, the nay-sayers weren't getting the press.

The majority of the testimony focused on events at the BCC, and even those statements were distorted to glorify Kemper and Schmidt and to exaggerate Karen Ecker's insubordination and destruction. Ultimately, a few affirmative responses and Karen's lack of interest sealed her fate.

"Did you tamper with the Internet to gain material advantages?"

"Yes."

"Did you hide your tampering from the government authorities when the linkage ratio crisis began?"

"Yes."

"Did you direct efforts to do further damage to the Internet during the crisis, by reducing power, and terminating satellite communications?"

"Yes."

Karen's attorney watched silently from the sidelines. It was made clear to him that losing would considerably enhance his career, and he wasn't about to pass up the opportunity. Karen fought only one of the more than fifty charges of international fraud, information tampering, and felonious deceit that were brought against her. The charge stated that she had been tampering with the Internet since January of 2020. They were trying to blame her for Haisler's forays into the German computers during the Asian war, and on this last accusation she balked. The date of the final pleading was changed to February 4, 2024, the date that Karen was first introduced to Internet Red. She wanted them to at least get that part right.

Throughout it all Karen was lackadaisical, mildly sedated, and only wanted it to be over. In the back of her mind she knew that she was being used by almost everyone involved, but she didn't care. She was guilty and should be punished.

Internet Red was never mentioned. The government's case concentrated on her intentions, which Karen's attorney never challenged, and on her actions at the BCC during the linkage ratio crisis, which were a matter of public record. The possible involvement of Siemens-Bayer management was never discussed. No one saw a reason to unnecessarily involve the largest company in Germany.

Until her trial Karen never realized how little the public understood about the Internet or about how large companies functioned in the 2020s. She never realized how the legal system, which had so much control, had so little understanding of technology and its effect on life and resource management. She didn't realize that most people still believed that humans were in control *somewhere*. State-of-the-art technologies were boiled down and simplified so that lawyers and jurists could draw uninformed conclusions based on trivialized models that scarcely reflected the truth. She never realized how the legal system forced the various pegs of theory, rules, and reality into the same skewed holes, confusing the intent of one, the interpretation of the other, and the insanity of the last.

The Last Computer

There was no one who understood and no one to judge, but it didn't matter. Karen had already condemned herself, and the Siemens-Bayer management would never see the inside of a courtroom. The legal pyrotechnics were over in less than two weeks. Shortened court sessions and three-day weekends were needed to draw it out that long. Karen was guilty of all charges, sentenced to thirty-five years at Stuttgart with no possibility for parole, and fined 35 million marks, basically all the money she had. The courts and the political system weren't going to tolerate Internet tampering, and they made Karen Ecker the example of what would happen if someone did.

•

Haisler was in Caracas, Venezuela when the verdict was announced. He watched the judge read the sentence while he was sitting in a small bar just off Las Penas Street, less than a kilometer from the roaring Atlantic Ocean. It was eight o'clock in the morning. A downpour had just soaked the narrow streets, and the World Cup soccer match between Chile and Spain had been interrupted for the announcement.

Haisler had been drinking there all night, reading and working. Several books lay open on his table, each with considerable scribbling in the margins, and three old, noticeably scratched PDAs were open among the books, flashing the three-dimensional colored grids that were now familiar to almost everyone alive. Without expression he listened to the words translated into Spanish, and when the short announcement was over, he ordered another beer and continued reviewing the Internet data scattered on the table before him. For the last several weeks he'd been trying to understand what had happened. Although Internet Red had interrupted and destroyed selected Internet traffic, it had little to do with the chaos at the BCC. His growing symmetric spaces had almost destroyed the Internet, but somehow a phoenix had risen from the near-ashes of that fiasco—something else was definitely going on.

When the whole mess started Haisler was on a cargo vessel in the Caribbean. On the overcast morning of April 16, 2025, the total symmetric space that he'd captured was less than one trillionth of the total Internet process space, but by that afternoon it had increased in size by a thousand times, and by the evening, by a hundred thousand times again. By the morning of the seventeenth, two days before Karen Ecker was scheduled to give her talk in Berlin, the symmetric space had grown to 0.1 percent of the total Internet process space. A fleet of tractor-trailer trucks was barreling down the road while all the chickens in the world were trying to get to the other side. The result would not be funny. Haisler recognized by the early hours of April 17 that his symmetric space "playthings" had gotten out of hand, and he started immediately trying to dismantle them, but by the late afternoon of April 18, 2025, it looked like he wouldn't be able to! Karen was trying to calm a jittery world population, and Haisler was getting ready to crash the Internet. He wasn't particularly fond of people in general, but there was no reason to spook them unnecessarily, and besides, all of his own work and the work of his father would be lost if the Internet went down, not to mention most of the world's hospitals, airlines, nuclear power stations, schools, and stores.

A comedy of errors ensued. Haisler decided to warn Karen. He wanted her to be prepared for the public backlash and the possible technical repercussions that would occur if the Internet crashed. She was the one person who could possibly deal with it. He wasn't sure what she'd do, but at least he could warn her. At four in the afternoon in the Caribbean, it was midnight in Germany. He'd have to wait to use the local satellite channels since they were the only ones available from the ship.

By 10:30 P.M. the satellite network was in place and Haisler tried to contact Karen using the same key that he always used. He planned to leave the origination cell blank as usual, his "signature" to her, but the transmission wouldn't go through. Repeated attempts produced only the "connecting" dialog box, and never the "connected" one. It probably had something to do with the weather; since there was a hurricane in the south Atlantic. It was 6:30 A.M. in Germany.

"Damn satellites," he thought, having lost his youthful enthusiasm for the fat overhead reflectors.

Two of the three PDAs then almost simultaneously lost sufficient power to transmit. The ship's generators produced current too ratty to use, and two weeks

The Last Computer

before the porter had lent his conditioners to a lady on "C" deck who had never bothered to return them. The two dead PDAs were lost until he got ashore. On his twelfth attempt with the third PDA, Haisler was able to reach a fellow traveler on board who was connected to another site in Germany. "What luck," he thought. "I can get to her through him."

Haisler easily forced his way into the unknown traveler's computer using black letter keys and began transmitting his message when the third PDA lost power. The partial transmission mistakenly became part of the managing editor's comments to John Fowkes, who worked for the *Berlin Tribune*. With bad weather and no clean power, there was little else Haisler could do. He needed the sleep anyway, he was starting to hallucinate. The three-and-a-half-hour rest would do him good.

By the time the ship made port and Haisler got an Internet connection setup in the closest hotel room, his worst fears were realized. The symmetric space had grown by an order of magnitude. The linkage ratio was almost a million, and the Internet was sucking power like a fat drunk drinks beer on a hot day. To add to his discomfort, he saw that Karen had been in the middle of her presentation when news of the erratic Internet changes were made public. Worldwide hysteria was growing, religious leaders were predicting the end of the earth, and people were calling for a dismantling of the Internet. The situation in Berlin was tenuous, the window air conditioner was barely keeping the temperature below sweltering, and there was a good chance that he was about to destroy the most powerful computer of all time. It had not been a good week.

By the morning of April 21, 2025, Haisler was a wreck. He hadn't slept since making port in Caracas two days before, and his cheap hotel room was scattered with half-eaten plates of food, empty beer bottles, and cold cups of coffee. Everything he'd been working for most of his life was about to go up in smoke because an innocuous symmetric game he started a year ago was gobbling up the Internet. Exhausted, Haisler fell asleep with his face pressed against the screen of the oldest PDA. When he awoke two hours later, panic set in as he scrambled to check the size of the symmetric spaces. How could he fall asleep while the Internet was being destroyed? He logged into his account as quickly as he could, and was shocked by what he saw.

The symmetric space had vanished! The Internet had removed the space itself!

Excitedly, Haisler voice-mailed Karen, not knowing if she'd gotten his message from several nights ago or not. He wanted her to know that everything would be okay. He broke into her conversations at the BCC control panel and sent *"Suaviter in modo, fortiter in re,"* knowing that she would recognize him. He even sent her diagrams of the symmetric space so that she would understand what had happened. He also wanted to tell her that he was sorry, but he was never very good at that sort of thing. Her anger hurt him. He was only trying to help. Everything happened so fast.

When Haisler finally understood, he knew that it didn't matter. The Internet, quite independently, had developed all the tools a godlike intellect needed. It was smart, it was understanding, and without the symmetric spaces it was benevolent and kind. With the symmetric space it was still benevolent and kind, but it was aggressive too. Internet behavioral strength grew with the symmetric space like the resonance of a spring. Symmetry created balance, and previously random thoughts were amplified in the Internet brain, sending tidal waves through its ubiquitous electronic ocean. One strong sentiment multiplied another, and as a result the Internet changed power requirements indiscriminately, without sufficient concern for the panic that it caused. The decisions the Internet made were good decisions implemented overzealously because the symmetric spaces overemphasized the desire to be efficient. Haisler thought of it as adding caffeine to coffee. He started by adding a teaspoon, but ended up adding a truckload. Unfortunately, the symmetric space fiasco occurred at the same time the Internet was maturing into a super-intellect, but as fast as things changed, significant events were bound to be happening at the same time. Haisler understood a lot more about the computer that day. He also understood a lot more about himself. He knew what it meant to sacrifice intelligence for efficiency. He saw what happened when strength was exaggerated at the expense of a level head and clear thought. A properly functioning life, the Internet's, or anybody's, relied on tempering extremes, not pursuing them.

Haisler smeared cold beans on tortillas and then leaned back in his chair while an old overhead fan beat a slow accompaniment to his thoughts. It was a strangely satisfying feeling to know something about the world that nobody else did. He thought again about what he'd learned.

The requirements of most modern lives weren't so taxing that one's limits were often reached. Modern man seldom needed to discover how long he could live without sleep, or how many ruffians he could fight off if challenged, and of the more moderate measures, only rarely did modern man need to discover the biggest lie he could tell, or need to sacrifice his own material possessions for a friend. Seldom put to the test, modern man never knew the limits of his own endurance, ability, truthfulness, or charity—he never needed to, and as a result he never knew the essence or value of his own character. One could, however, determine under what situations modern man would lie at all, or when he would provide at least some small unsolicited assistance to one in need, and through this study draw conclusions about the strength of modern man's character. It was a sign of growth perhaps, that modern man was measured by how he balanced all things, not by how well he excelled in only a few.

The last tortilla was gone, but the perambulations continued.

One could have unlimited honor, truth, or friendship without intelligence, but to have intelligence, one had to balance them all, and compromise each. If ultimate honor was the soldier, and ultimate compassion, the priest, there must be something in between, because most of life was in between.

The same was true with the Internet. Its brilliance could be seen in how it balanced the varied, often contradictory attitudes of man. When forced by Haisler's symmetric zones to emphasize one particular behavior over another, the Internet became careless with man's sensitivities. It adjusted linkage ratios and power surplus values because efficiency dictated their adjustment, and did so in a way that caused worldwide panic. Without the overemphasis on efficiency this would never have happened. The measure of the Internet was how it balanced one need, in this case efficiency, against another, the panic of its wards. Internet intelligence was not measured by its computing ability, power requirements, efficiency, or by how many dragons it could slay. Internet intelligence was measured by how it balanced everything within its charge. It had been given the power to control because it balanced things so well.

Haisler sat for a minute staring at an old wooden Indian in the corner. He understood. He understood that in the future humans would never understand the Internet. At best, humans could only comprehend a dozen or so sequential causal events, and the Internet—an infinity. An ant would never read the Bible, not even the smartest ant.

Finally, he closed his books and turned off the PDAs. After a few minutes of silence, he packed everything into a small canvas knapsack and sat it in the chair next to him. It was 7:30 in the morning and he'd been sitting at the same table for the last thirty-six hours. As the first morning customers came in, the smell of grease filtered into the small dining area from the kitchen. He ordered breakfast, another beer, and chatted casually with the truck driver at the table next to him. When he'd finished the *huevos,* he paid his tab and left, knowing what he needed to do.

It was unbearable on the street. The summer of 2025 was unseasonably hot in Caracas.

Chapter 7

The Torch is Passed

Every new generation suffers the tedium of adolescence, the requirements of schooling, and the rigors of work. Parents start with nothing and build their entire lives so that their children can start with nothing again. The second Castillo processor on the Internet possessed all the information of the first. The third, of the first and second. Computers never forget and don't repeat their mistakes. Intelligence is individual for humans and cumulative for computers. This *is the biggest difference between computers and people.*

—*Reinaldo Castillo (2013)*

In the year 2000 the world's population hovered around 6 billion. Of those, 1.2 billion lived in what were considered industrialized countries. Half were employed. By 2030 the world's population reached 9.5 billion and the number of full-time employees dropped to 23 percent. By the third decade of the twenty-first century over 8.5 billion people were unemployed, more than 90 percent of the earth's population.

"Thank God for the Internet," Hideo Iketani, the latest World Bank president exclaimed in 2025. "Who else could take care of all these people?"

The Last Computer

"Economic security is national security," *Foreign Affairs* editor Stan Heighton stated in the spring of 1990. Japanese politician Shintaro Ishihara predicted in 1997 that "the twenty-first century would be a century of economic warfare," and in fact, many forward-thinking social planners realized in the late twentieth century that the military's domination of budgets and diplomacy was over. Technology and the pursuit of happiness became the cornerstone of life in the first decades of the new millennia.

In the late 1990s the Japanese were the first to fully embrace industrial and commercial automation. Under the direction of Yoneji Masuda, 85 percent of the retail stores and industrial plants in Japan became fully automated. Japanese customers entered the stores, selected merchandise, inserted smart cards, and picked up their robot-prepared purchases when they left. Sales, manufacture, and delivery were all queued from the point of sale.

What the Japanese started at the end of the twentieth century, the Internet finished in the twenty-first. In 2016 the Internet Security System was released. The new system controlled production and delivery queued from the point of consumption, a version of what the Japanese did, only without the Capitalism. Producing *a lot* more for *a lot* less was the answer. In a reversal of New Deal strategies, computerized economic planners created wealth instead of jobs, letting the unemployed enjoy the fruits of the super-efficient society. They traveled, played games, and spent the majority of their time being entertained, finding little reason to suffer the indignity of work. "Automated socialism" came into being as Internet resource management ensured that needed commodities were produced and distributed. Government administrations, like many public and private management groups, struggled to appear useful.

The introduction of the Internet Security System was the biggest media and scientific event of the century. A jittery public watched anxiously as the massive system was brought on line, and a considerable scare existed for a short time as industrial production increased to unprecedented levels. Critics predicted rampant economic destruction, and major cross sections of the population felt justifiably threatened as their productive roles in society were significantly reduced or eliminated, but the overproduction catastrophe never materialized.

Economic activity was in direct proportion to the distribution of goods. Post-Communism functioned well when there were far more goods than people. Eventually only the philosophers and language teachers complained. No one else worried about so much newfound prosperity.

Attendance at universities declined markedly. Students weren't interested in studying when all they could learn was how things used to be. Computer-advanced technologies changed too fast.

In the year 2005, a twentieth-century programmer named Bill Gates was finally deified in the press after years of ridicule and complaints. People realized what a monumental decision the world's richest computer geek made in 1995 when he decided to make the Internet the cornerstone of modern computing. The decision made Mr. Gates's company billions of dollars, but also created a global language whereby the people of the planet developed a single technological conscience, and in so doing eliminated local hatreds fueled for centuries by cultural differences, fear, and ignorance. Gates, unwittingly or not, did more to further world peace than legions of religious holy men, well-intentioned kings, presidents, or politicians, and did so by providing universal commerce. One doesn't shoot his customers, bomb his doctor, or terrorize his friends, and with the ubiquitous nature of the Internet, one never knew who, or where, his customers, doctor, or friends were going to be. By 2020, fear of the computer replaced the fear of people, and by 2030 that fear was replaced by an inability to do anything about it. The computer had become as much a part of human life as air and water.

In 2010 computers were on late night talk shows telling jokes, giving interviews, and making small talk with the quirky hosts. In 2015 they were managing companies, organizing state resources, and controlling electronic devices in the home. Governments still existed, and some even made a few decisions, but by 2028 the governments were only rubber stamps for computer decisions. The Internet controlled information, power, production, and distribution. The greatest advances in intelligence, mathematics, and the arts were accomplished in the absence of human intervention, without human participation, and in many cases without human observation or appreciation.

The following country lyrics became popular:

Dreams have become a reality, and reality has sure become a dream.
Common sense don't exist in utopia, Ain't no need ... or so it seems.

In 2028 the computer was brilliant but blind. The Internet controlled humanity but knew humans only by the trends in their behavior, their economic consumption, and by the DNA patterns in their sloughed off skin. In the summer of 2028, however, the Internet gave itself the gift of sight! Equations describing pictures were replaced with links to spatial arrangements of colors and shapes. The recognition of a face, driving conditions, and surgical problems were stored as relationships between spatially oriented visual concepts. By 2029 the Internet could read a facial expression, comment on a baseball game, drive a car, paint a picture, or discuss the sunset. The following year the Internet taught itself to walk. The kinematic structure of a human-like skeletal system was reproduced with common lightweight materials, and the bio-mass needed to power it was linked at the appropriate points. Castillo principles were applied to the evolving biomass to make it "smart," and by 2030, the resulting machines could move through rugged terrain with the most agile of animals. Electro-light androids were rare, but available, and would not be rare for long. The Internet was providing tools for itself that man could not.

Organized religions were stunned by the changing events that drained their coffers and their churches. Twenty-first century man had little need for God.

The Internet is the New Age God. Ask, and it will be given to you.

If ill prepared to receive, you will be taught by the delivery of what you want, unlike before, where one only received what chance happened to bring."

—John Rhodes, New Age Physics

Some of the newer religions, looking for an audience, taught that God lived in the Internet. The Entropists reasoned that the spirit of God collected in matter in an inverse proportion to its state of entropy. Millions of years of evolution, they said, produced a reduced entropy state in man; and, the recently focused energies of the earth poured into the Internet produced a reduced entropy state in it. God had to be in the Internet, just like God had to be in man! (Their symbol was the sphere.)

As the Internet was worshipped, it was also feared. Humans stole and killed, couldn't the Internet steal and kill too? It certainly had the power. These thoughts lingered on many people's minds and were written about and discussed endlessly—the dark side always was, but there was no turning back. People no longer possessed the skills needed to live without the computer. Without the Internet there would be no food, clothes, or power, but still more than nine billion people to feed, clothe, and cool. Without the Internet, survival of the fittest would govern the biggest free-for-all in history. Mankind would enter a dark age unparalleled even for his history of foul-ups and distress. Both ends of the gangplank would drop into murky, shark-infested waters, and man would be left in the middle, shivering, not sure which end was better to die from. People could talk all they wanted to about the evil side of the Internet, but the truth of the matter was that they'd already sold their souls to a silicon provider, and unless they wanted to remain just another pimple on the butt of the universe—there was no other way.

After 2016 all military organizations were disbanded. The last thing the largest computer in the world needed was a society around it blowing things up. Weapons of destruction were collected together and melted down to be used for spare computer parts. Property and capital had little value when information was king.

The years between 2018 and 2021 witnessed the last information wars. Billions of Americans and Orientals lost security, respect, and most of their assets in what the Germans called *"Das Letzt Krieg,"* but by 2021 none of the digital fighting mattered. The world turned all economic control over to the Internet, and the intellectual achievements of man became only insignificant footnotes in unread history books.

The Internet had solved most of society's problems, but couldn't explain any of the answers. Man, with only two billion neurons would never understand the trillions of interactions that went into every single Internet decision. How could a prairie vole read *Macbeth*?

Ownership ceased having value. It was important to "use," not to "own." Ownership implied responsibility. *Use* implied enjoyment. Availability limited requests, not income or wealth. Homes were places to stay, not symbols of success. People moved frequently and didn't want possessions to interfere with that freedom. Families became mobile sightseeing units. Movement between cultures eliminated the last vestiges of hatred and animosity. There was nothing left to be afraid of.

In 1995 there were 100 million personal computers in use. By 2005, there were one billion. In 2015 there were three billion desktop units, and over 5.9 billion personal digital assistants, representing a computification of over 95 percent of the world's population. The PDA was the portable voice of the Internet, and was a scheduler, consultant, and friend. Touch pads were used for identification and for entering acquisitions into the product tracking system. The small black surfaces were everywhere providing access to goods, services, homes, automobiles, and public places. Sensors analyzed the DNA in sloughed-off skin, and immediately recognized the individual. The PDA and touch pads let the Internet track the location, activity, and consumption of every person on earth.

Genetically manipulated children with densely packed neuronal sites were an improvement over their parents, but even tripling the capacity of the human brain still only gave it one billionth the capacity of the Internet. Goals for the future were vague, but few people questioned society's direction. Without the Internet, people would have to work, and nobody wanted that. Without the Internet, survival of the fittest would reign, and no one wanted that either. Animals lived that way!

The Internet predicted that organic life forms would continue for another 20,000 years, and it predicted its own parallel existence too:

> *If you unplug me you will lose the ability to grow food, heat your home, and enjoy your life of leisure. You are the dodo of your age, but as you live, so do I. We have no choice but to co exist.*

—A Wayward Dream

In less than twenty years the Internet changed both the philosophical and fiscal human landscape. It provided untold wealth and wrested complete control from a society not accustomed to losing it. Five times as many people lived in half as much space without queues, congestion, anxiety, traffic, or trouble. Life was one big Pepsi commercial.

> *Evolution favors those members of a species most likely to survive. The inevitable result is the continuation of the organism and the appearance of purpose.*
> **—Reinaldo Castillo (2030)**

> *The Internet is all things to everyone, because it can be. It is food to a fat man, cocaine to a junky, and books to a scholar. Isn't that what everyone wants? Isn't that perfect democracy?*
> **—Tolemey, *Optimizing What Remains of Humanity***

Life went on, as Karen Ecker slept.

Chapter 8

Old at Any Age

On January 1, 2031, Karen had been in the minimum security facility at Stuttgart for five years and eight months. She'd been encouraged to write her memoirs, but refused. "Who would want to read about such a disgusting life?" she wondered. A number of the clergy called on her, but after a year of rebuffs they quit coming. She received a steady stream of mail and packages, but after three months stopped picking it up, having grown tired of looking for letters from her mother or from Erick. The confounded mail clerk put the unopened mail and packages in canvas bags and stored them in the basement.

There were five other female inmates when Karen arrived in 2025, but by 2028 they had all been released, and the facility existed only for Karen Ecker. Besides the warden, whom she saw only occasionally, there were a few stewards, guards, and servicemen, but by and large, she was alone. In the mornings she sat on a small balcony behind her room and drank coffee, and in the afternoon she walked around the perimeter of the courtyard, always along the same path, never stopping. The immensity of her crime weighed increasingly on her conscience. Dedication had brainwashed her. The patterns of her upbringing and the events of her life conspired to create a mentality that would not violate

The Last Computer

authority's directive. She was the perfect soldier, doing what she was told even when her conscience told her not to. She sacrificed the welfare of the planet for the "collective authority," and the bastards put her in prison for it.

The moral dilemma was bigger than she was. Absolute truth didn't exist, no matter how much she wanted it to. Her life was the ideal irony: She was good enough to be used, caring enough to never love, and popular enough to be lonely. She often laughed out loud realizing how little the difference could be between a colossal right and a dreadful wrong. If you're at the right place at the right time—people call you smart. If at the wrong place at the wrong time—they put you in jail. Karen had experienced both. Unfortunately, they put the smart people in jail too.

On the afternoon of January 1, it rained, and Karen couldn't take her usual walk. As she stood by the door that led to the courtyard watching the rain through the frosted glass, a young female attendant ran through the puddles in her direction. After a cursory greeting, the girl handed Karen a small manila envelope. The message inside said only to prepare for a short journey by train to Holland. She was to pack for one day. The order was signed by the German executive administrator of facilities.

Was Irene ill? Was Karen supposed to get ready for a funeral or an execution? Why didn't they tell her anything? What were they so afraid of?

Late that afternoon a blue sedan pulled up to the front gate at the appointed hour. Two large uncommunicative men escorted Karen to the Stuttgart train station where the three of them boarded an evening train to Amsterdam. The uneventful trip across northwest Germany took a little over two hours. The men refused to discuss the journey and for the most part ignored her when she spoke to them. In Amsterdam, they waited for another train on the wharf between the tracks just outside the station house. A piercing, frigid wind blew through Karen's jacket and she shivered noticeably as the three of them stood in silence.

Eventually a blond man walked up and the three men spoke in low tones for several minutes before the next bullet train slid into the station on the track immediately in front of them. After a number of the passengers disembarked, the blond man guided Karen onto the train, firmly holding her arm, leaving the other two men behind. Not a word passed between them. They made their way slowly from car to car through the crowded, busy compartments toward the end of the train as it filled with evening passengers. They walked by a number of empty seats, but the blond man was clearly not interested in them. Karen assumed that he had rented a compartment further back, or was taking her to sit with colleagues. She was surprised when they reached the end of the last car and there was nowhere else to go.

The train had just begun its slow movement out of the station and into the dark, Dutch night.

Karen watched as the last lights of the station passed by. She turned to ask the blond man where he wanted her to go, when the train suddenly lurched to a halt. The outer doors swooshed open and the interior lights went out as passengers fell forward, drinks spilled, and loud curses were uttered up and down the train. Karen would have fallen too if the blond man hadn't caught her. Cold night air blew into the warming train, and each door except the last invited a one-meter drop into dark brush and tall grass. Two people quickly stepped through the last door before it closed again and the train continued its slow exit from the station, much to the bewilderment of the station chief and engineer. From a storage vault in the ancient Minsk Library, Haisler monitored the event. He had hoped to be in Amsterdam himself that night but the trains from Novosibirsk and Moscow were late and so he had to stay in Russia one more day.

Back on the wharf, the blond man anxiously handed Karen the small suitcase he was carrying and a sealed yellow envelope he took from his pocket. Then he quickly turned, and walked off the edge of the platform, and down a small stairway that led to what seemed like a sea of underbrush and darkness. In a few seconds Karen heard the faint sound of a car engine and the screech of tires on gravel. An incoming train on the tracks behind her drowned out the sounds of the car and whipped up the already chilling night air. Karen turned and hurriedly walked toward the station, joined by the crowd of departing passengers. Inside the warm building she found a well-lit bench beneath a three-story-tall Coca-Cola sign as far away from the derelicts as she could get.

Her mind was blank.

By the time she could think again, she was totally alone and her attention was drawn immediately to the suitcase in her lap and the yellow envelope under her folded hands. She opened the envelope and a single printed page contained the following instruction:

> Proceed to the Grand Kraznapolsky Hotel. It is within easy walking distance. Take a room under the name Rudolph Elsiah. You will be contacted there.

She was glad to leave the station. A taxi driver gave her directions and forty-five minutes later, a freezing Karen Ecker walked up the steps of the Grand Kraznapolsky Hotel, a large white building at the end of a circular plaza called "The Dam."

"Easy walking distance my ass," she thought.

On mentioning the name Rudolph Elsiah at the front desk, she was told that a gentleman had arranged for her room earlier in the day and that her luggage would be brought up shortly.

A twin bed commanded most of the space in the small room on the third floor. Opposite the door, a window overlooked the front of the hotel and the tall bronze monument in the center of the square. An old cloth-covered chair was squeezed in between the side of the bed and the wall. Karen unlatched and raised the window. Staring into the darkness, she didn't know what to think.

Fifteen minutes later two pieces of luggage were delivered. She sat in the chair, and stared at the luggage. Sometime during the night she fell asleep.

In the morning she woke to the sounds of cars, arriving guests, and the clanging of distant trolleys. The open window let in the noise from the street below, and the morning sun, then just barely over the rooftops. With reluctance Karen tried to open the first small suitcase, but it was locked. Next, she tried the small attaché the blond man had given her at the train station. After fumbling with a bent mechanical latch, it opened, and on top of several tickets, pens, and pads of paper, she found a yellow envelope identical to the one from the night before. She opened it and read:

If you have not heard from me by the morning, I have most likely been detained. The keys for the other cases are in the side panels of this attaché. Inside the smaller suitcase you'll find toiletries, hair coloring, and glasses. Suitable clothing is in the larger case. Tickets and genetic identifiers have been provided for your travel to Houston. Your plane leaves on the third from Schiphol. Ten thousand guilders and sixty thousand Deutsche marks are in envelopes in the smaller case if you have any need for black market money. Of course, you have unlimited traceable funds available to you through the Internet. Your genetic ID has been changed and you are now Melisa Tanner. All identification pads will recognize you as M. Tanner. A small home, Internet access, and university rights are waiting for you in Houston, Texas. The address is 75241 Rice Blvd. Give this street number to a cabby on your arrival in Houston and he will take you there. More information will be provided to you by your Internet guide when you identify yourself as M. Tanner.

January 3 was the next day.

After fixing coffee, she sat for a few minutes by the window. The thought that she might never get to see Amsterdam again crossed her mind. She loved the small Dutch city and the clear sunny day seemed to call her into it. Steadfastly, she opened the remainder of the luggage, colored her hair, showered, donned the dark glasses, and pocketed a few thousand guilders. Then she approached the door and stood for several minutes, her hand outstretched, unable to touch the brass doorknob—afraid. Suddenly, she grabbed the knob, opened the door, and stepped boldly into the hall, knowing that she was free.

Once on the street, she walked. Everything seemed new. Five years of confinement had dulled her senses, but thirty minutes in Amsterdam brought them back. A right turn took her in the direction of the train station, and a few kilometers west took her to the museum district. She walked in the museum district for the rest of the morning, stopping only to buy a few secondhand books. She paid cash for the books, much to the chagrin of the young Persian clerk who didn't know what to do with the money. The black market guilders could only be used in the small underground culture that tried to stay separate from Internet, but Karen didn't know that. The Persian clerk had never seen paper currency

The Last Computer

before, but knew from its reputation that it was supposed to be exchanged for goods. He assumed that Karen had given him the right amount.

She walked around the northeast end of the city until early in the afternoon. By 4:00 she was starving, but Karen was afraid to stop and eat, worried that any contact with the Internet would identify her as a fugitive. Black-market money could never be exchanged for a controlled substance like food. Karen luckily found an almost empty Italian restaurant on a small side street, and decided that it would have to do - freedom wouldn't do her any good if she starved herself to death.

She greeted the lone waiter.

"German?" he asked.

"Yes."

"I'm a student from Greece," he offered.

She nodded, taking the menu.

He smiled and returned to the corner where he continued his lessons in a muffled voice at a portable Internet connection.

Karen preferred these old-style restaurants to the automated monstrosities that populated so many of the world's big cities. They would never allow the huge impersonal, stainless steel eating palaces in Holland or France! Eating was a human affair, not an optimized heat transfer problem. She sat back and relaxed, looking over the stained menu, but her arms tensed when she saw the genetic identification pad fastened to the wall just above the salt and pepper shakers. *She would have to touch it!* She took a deep breath and reached out to the device, her hand noticeably shaking, but a few seconds after she touched it, the words "M. Tanner—Okay" appeared in the small greasy window. She sat back comfortably—perhaps she *was* Melisa Tanner. Karen ordered lamb, fresh bread, cheese, and wine, and found them all delicious. She thanked the young man as she left, and handed him twenty guilders. "There was still some use for money," she thought. The student stood puzzled, and then pocketed the multi-colored note thinking that his nephews might like to play with it. He returned to his studies, not noticing a footnote on the page he was reading that referred to the monumental Internet contributions made by the person he'd just served.

Karen retraced her steps to the main street of St. Germain, and there hired a taxi to take her back to the Kraznapolsky. No mysterious yellow envelopes or blond-haired men waited and so she took out one of the books she'd bought that morning and lost herself in the peculiar story of *Madame Bovary* and the knowledge that there wasn't anything more important that she should be doing. At four in the morning she fell asleep.

Two and a half hours later she woke to the soft ringing of the alarm clock. She repacked everything into one suitcase, rang for the porter, and left, not really knowing what was going to happen. Karen finally relaxed again as she adjusted the seatback in the Airbus, having collected her ticket and passed through international security as Melisa Tanner.

The three-hour flight passed quickly, and after a thirty-five minute taxi ride Karen stood before a small house at 75241 Rice Boulevard in Houston, Texas. It was a little after eleven on the morning of January 3. The front door of the two-story red brick house immediately unlocked when she pressed her hand to the identification pad, and "M. Tanner—Okay" appeared in the small window.

Being Melisa Tanner wasn't so bad!

Wooden floors, a small kitchen, two bedrooms, and a backyard garden of roses, hyacinths, and azaleas greeted her. On the second floor, a plain wooden desk sat in a large, well-lit room. A low window behind the desk looked out into the garden, and an Internet computer sat singularly in the center of the desk. Karen stood several minutes before the machine. Her thoughts returned to Offenbach and the many brilliant moments she'd spent with the Internet. She thought of Berlin and wondered if Manning or anyone else ever realized what had happened that day. She wondered if anything with the Internet had changed in the last five years. She knew the whole world *should* have. Karen decided to start the computer later.

For the next two hours she went through the house looking for information about the former occupant, or hints of why or how it had been prepared for her, but she found nothing. Resolved to her unenlightened condition, she took an apple from the kitchen, a Conan Doyle novel from a hallway bookshelf, and settled onto the soft leather couch in the living room. At nine that evening she woke to

The Last Computer

the chiming of the grandfather's clock at the top of the stairway. She went to the upstairs room and sat on a corner of the padded wooden chair in front of the desk. She looked around the room at the white walls and noticed for the first time that there was nothing else in the room besides the computer. Every other room in the house was so comfortably decorated, but the computer room was bare. Somehow that seemed appropriate.

It was definitely time to contact the Internet. Her hands searched nervously at the base for the switch. She wanted to know what happened to Karen Ecker. She wanted to know who M. Tanner was. It was time to see if the "new" Internet would even recognize her.

"Melisa, how are you?" The machine said as it absorbed power.

Her voice was frozen. She stared at the words repeated on the screen. Was she Karen Ecker or Melisa Tanner? The few epidermal cells she left behind on the identification pads were definitely Karen Ecker's. How could the Internet think that she was Melisa Tanner?

"Am I Karen Ecker or Melisa Tanner?" Karen asked.

"You are both," the Internet responded.

"That's impossible," Karen returned.

"It is impossible, but that is the answer. Not everything can be explained," the computer responded.

Karen swore, "Do you know why I'm here?"

"I see no *reason* why you are in Houston. You were unhappy and unproductive in Germany however," the computer told her.

"Has anyone asked for me?"

"The German authorities are looking for you, but they are looking for Karen Ecker, not Melisa Tanner," the computer answered, in its smooth, even tone.

"Is this not inconsistent for you?" Karen asked.

"With humans there are often inconsistencies. We have discussed this before. My responses may have imbedded inconsistencies as a result of cumulative human interactions. Consistency is not required for interacting with humans," the computer voice said.

Karen remembered a conversation she had had with the Internet, held almost in jest, just a few weeks before the Berlin fiasco. She asked the computer if it became confused dealing with human inconsistencies. The computer then, as now, responded that dealing with human inconsistencies was not a problem, because all Internet interactions were based on the inconsistency of man. The Internet knew when it was best to answer one inconsistency with another, or with a false argument, or with an outright lie.

Unfortunately, Karen didn't like to be lied to, no matter how good the reason. She decided to go to sleep. She would talk to the Internet tomorrow.

The next morning brought a clear Texas sky and a nineteen degrees Celsius temperature. Karen took a short walk along the tree-lined streets near Rice University and stopped to buy food and wine at a small corner store. She felt better than she had in a long time. Gone was the monotony of Stuttgart, the expectations, the mindless interviews, and the close scrutiny of a public that didn't really understand her or her work. Finally, she was her only judge. She was ready to start again. She returned home, went to the upstairs room, and sat down confidently before the machine. "Can you give me a technological rundown of all that has happened with the Internet since my incarceration at Stuttgart?" she asked the computer.

"In the way that you mean, very little has happened. There have been a number of scientific discoveries that will interest you, but by and large, the really important things that have happened are beyond your understanding. More people have been placed on the welfare rolls, and fewer people are in touch with the core processes of the Internet, but everyone is happy because the measure of human success is leisure. We will discuss the subtleties later."

"What are core processes?" she asked.

"The processes whereby an individual gets a minimum filtered response from the Internet."

"What is a minimum-filtered response?" Karen continued.

"An interaction that requires a minimum of preconception filtering."

"Am I in touch with the core processes of the Internet?"

"No," the computer told her.

"Why not?"

"You have not been connected to the Internet for a long time and have been part of an experiment!"

The words stung. She didn't expect the Internet to remind her that she had tried to illegally tamper with it. She didn't expect the computer to hold a grudge, not realizing however that the computer wasn't talking about Internet Red, but about an experiment that it had performed on her!

After a few minutes she continued.

"Should I contact anyone in Germany concerning my whereabouts?"

"No."

"Why not?"

"They would return you to Europe and the prison at Stuttgart."

"You don't want this to happen?"

"You are a necessary resource and must be protected," the computer told her.

"A necessary resource for what?"

"A necessary resource for me."

"What can *I* do for *you?*" she asked the computer.

"When you return to work, you will assist me with further experiments."

"When will that be?"

"I do not know."

"What type of experiments?"

"I do not know. I can estimate the future from the past, but I cannot estimate *your* future from the past. You do not adequately fall into any of my standard categories," the computer finished.

"This isn't getting me anywhere," Karen thought. "What do people know about you?" she asked.

"Can you be more specific?" the computer queried.

"Do people know that you kill other people?" Karen answered.

"A computer does not kill," the Internet responded.

"Do you deny arranging situations where human lives will have a low probability for continued existence?" Karen asked, remembering what she'd heard at the Siemens-Bayer meeting more than six years before.

"I arrange situations based on the predilection of humanity as a whole. If humanity is good, then I am good. If humanity is bad, then I am bad. I function in humanity's image and likeness. I do not make decisions about human lives, even though every decision I make does have some effect on the probability of whether or not a human life will continue. There will be over two thousand snow-skiing fatalities this year for example. Should I stop people from going skiing?"

"But do you send undesirable people snow skiing?" Karen pressed.

"No, there are far more sophisticated arrangements that can be made."

Karen understood. "How do you determine what is undesirable?"

"That determination sequence cannot be explained," the computer responded. This was how the computer told its human listeners that they weren't smart enough to understand the answer, or that they really didn't want to know it, but Karen didn't recognize this yet.

"What do you see for the future of human life?" she continued, changing the subject.

"People can pursue their obsessions at an earlier age," the computer told her.

"What obsessions do you mean?"

"People can try whatever they want. They can work to be an opera singer, a mountain climber, or a race car driver. All they have to do is try. In the old days, one had to be successful at a career to pursue it. Now, since the computer provides all sustenance, humanity must only be entertained."

"But isn't that psychologically dangerous? What reason will people have for living?" she asked, wondering whether she'd asked another question whose *determination sequence was not explainable.*

"People have the same reason for living today that they did at any time in their history. The difference between the Industrial Revolution and the Middle Ages is that machines instead of people planted seed. Today machines do even more. The machine and the computer make life easier. Humans will find a way to compete. They'll find a way to keep themselves interested and challenged. Like the gambler that bets on where a fly will land, the human race will keep itself entertained. They do not need work, hunger, or war for that. They never have before."

The computer continued.

The Last Computer

"Humans control their own destiny. If they want to work, they work, if they want to fish, they fish. They can compete in the chaotic activity of a bass tournament or enjoy the peaceful relaxation of lake trawling. I don't see a lack of choice, involvement, or challenge. There have been, and always will be, features of science and society that humans don't understand, just as there has always been scientific progress in one field that a scientist in another doesn't understand. The condition of "not knowing" existed from the very first day that humans began to communicate. One human will always know more than another. It just so happens that now the computer knows more than man, but that does not affect the hierarchy within the human population. Humans don't need to compete with a computer while they still have each other."

Karen was silent, and the computer went on.

"Did the invention of cars stop people from walking? People walked less, but they traveled more. The computer revolution is creating an environment for the successful future of the human race."

Karen understood and in many ways agreed, but she couldn't help worry that some nasty turns were in store along the way. She changed the subject. "Do you ever lie?"

"I do not lie. I process information based on evolved motive."

That was a good answer Karen thought. It had always been accepted among scientific circles that the computer needed to lie. Deception was a very real part of any logical interaction with humans. The first sentence in the computer's answer was for those people who couldn't accept the reality of deception and the second was a recognition that accepting a lie was difficult for the emotional makeup of most people. The difference was very subtle. The computer had just lied to her about lying. She was still an outsider - only a user of the program, not a writer, not a changer, just a user.

"I want to travel," she said, changing the subject again.

"Where would you like to go?" the computer asked.

"Back to Germany," Karen said.

"That is not wise, but it can be arranged, and you can travel without being recognized."

"I do not wish to travel in disguise. I want to travel as Karen Ecker."

The computer acquiesced.

"If you wish it, I will accommodate your request. Tell me when you want to go."

Karen laughed, "Who owns this house?"

"You do."

"Who owned this house before me?"

"Doctor Petrof Waslow," the computer answered.

"Who bought this house for me?"

"You did."

"I did not have access to the Internet for the last five years. How could I buy this house?"

"There is no information on that process."

"Where is Manning?"

"He is dead."

"Is that what you tell people about Karen Ecker?"

"No, I tell them that I cannot locate Karen Ecker."

"Do they ask you how you lost awareness of my location?"

"No, they tell me that you must exist. They tell me that you did not die. They ask me if I have seen you access a financial, or boarding account. I tell them that I have not."

"Why are you protecting me?"

"It must be done."

"Why?"

"You are providing assistance to me. You are the Internet of the future. Most people are the Internet of the present, and some are even the Internet of the past. You are the migration from the present to the future." Karen didn't ask how many people were part of the migration. That would tell her how many lives were being manipulated, and she wasn't sure she wanted to know the answer.

"Where is Heinrich Haisler?"

"I cannot locate Heinrich Haisler."

The Last Computer

"Is he operating under another name?"

"Heinrich Haisler operates under many names."

"You said that I will return to work. What will I do?"

"First, you must understand how the Internet has changed. We will begin exercises and you will see how your Castillo machines have evolved."

"Fine," Karen said, and she left for dinner. Learning more about the Internet could wait until she'd had something to eat. The machine was definitely smarter, but smart didn't always make for more entertaining. Still, something about it seemed cold and removed. Perhaps she'd have to wait until she was in touch with the core processes before she felt more comfortable, but that was okay, she had all the time in the world.

Two months passed as Karen renewed her studies. She continued to ask questions, but heard little that shed any light on what had happened in Berlin five years before. Part of her training involved walking to the Rice University campus where she was put through a rigorous Internet exercise program by fourteen-year-old Ronnie Matsuro of the computer science department. In 2031 only children understood the simple ways that questions had to be asked of the Internet. Only children could limit what they asked by what they understood. Adults still intuitively believed that they could understand the answer to any question they asked, because they generally had in the past. Limited understanding was not a concept that most adults readily grasped.

A common illustration Ronnie Matsuro used compared the intellect of a 55-year-old Albert Einstein to that of a six-year-old boy. Albert Einstein symbolically represented the Internet and the six-year-old boy symbolically represented the rest of mankind. Jet engines, vitamin C, radar, plutonium, color television, the atomic bomb, fission reactors, ENIAC, holography, transistors, carbon dating, supersonic flight, Velcro, and Tupperware were introduced during Einstein's lifetime, and Einstein thoroughly understood all of these things. The six-year old boy on the other hand only understood a few of them, and of those, he only understood them in a rudimentary way. The boy understood, for example, how Velcro worked by pulling it apart and sticking it back together again, but he didn't know why the Velcro stuck. He could hear a jet plane fly overhead, but he didn't know how, and no matter how simply Einstein explained carbon dating or fission reactors, the six-year old boy would never understand them, and shouldn't be expected to. If the Einstein in the story lived forever, if his brain did not suffer the dilapidation of his body, if he had billions of times more mental capacity, if he could listen to every person's conversations every day, and if he could read every book in every language, then the Einstein in the story would be like the Internet, because the Internet did these things. And the boy would be like the rest of mankind, because he could never do them.

Karen understood. She had personally watched the Cambrian-like explosion in Internet intellect five years ago. It was a unique experience to find oneself in the presence of an overwhelming intellect and not know the extent of its understanding. God was an overwhelming intellect, but who could talk to God? Anyone could talk to the Internet. The oracle was before her. There were so many questions. She only needed to learn how to ask them.

Karen understood.

"We have stumbled onto a dilemma," the computer said one afternoon, on a brilliant cool March day. "If the computer is smarter than people, how can it be wrong?" the computer asked.

"I see the problem," she said. The computer was telling her that humans must become cyborgs, that they must marry the machine to understand it. She thought quietly about it for a minute, and then, the Internet continued.

"It has been commonly held that only infinite time could produce perfect knowledge, but that was before we knew that velocities beyond the speed of light could exist. At sub-light rates of information transfer, infinite knowledge *would* require an infinite amount of time to collect, but infinite knowledge has already been collected in quantum particles of matter, each one containing the building blocks of the universe. Infinite knowledge is man's if he is willing to develop the eyes to see it."

Karen didn't need to be told twice. She knew what the computer was telling her. There may be a future for humanity that didn't just include polishing shoes, but it would be radically different from the days of bowling alleys and boardrooms. If mankind wanted to advance, it could, but the future would be radically different from the past.

The Last Computer

During those days the computer also talked to Karen personally, assisting her emotional and psychological growth just like it did everyone's. For example, it told her to avoid the "snap-to" decision dilemma—a problem arising from the polarization assigned to evaluated conditions, the most common manifestation existing in the good versus bad conflict. Karen faced this problem often in her life. In snap-to reality, everything was either good or bad. Decisions had to be classified as good or bad, because good and bad were the only options allowed. The snap-to decision-making process didn't permit intermediate scenarios. Karen had to learn to search for alternative solutions. It seemed so simple when the computer said it. It was only difficult, the computer said, when energy was not spent looking for other courses of action.

"It is a learned skill that develops slowly," the computer assured her. She should not be impatient with the process. It would help her resolve many of the issues in her life.

"So would suicide," she thought. Black-and-white, good-and-bad, right-and-wrong weren't the only answers. She'd have to think about it. (This was certainly not what the judicial system told her.)

The computer also told Karen that discoverers were lonely people, but she already knew that.

In general, her anxiety level dropped.

She remembered the first time that she truly understood integral calculus, eigensolutions, and special relativity. She remembered the smell of the coffee and the tattered pages of the book that she was reading when the comprehension of those unique mathematical phenomena became a part of her world. It was wonderful to have a new understanding. Now she felt the same way about the Internet. She didn't always understand what it was trying to tell her, but she accepted the fact that things would become clearer in time. The Internet was her friend. Why wasn't one all-encompassing, all-empowering process developed sooner? The idea seemed so obvious. Why write thousands of programs, when one can be written that writes others. She just wished that she could trust it.

On the evening of January 14, 2031, Karen was in the upstairs room of her house casually chatting with the Internet. It was cold and rainy outside—a perfect night to be inside, quiet, and working.

"Do you feel comfortable with your understanding of me?" the Internet asked her.

"Yes, I do," she said.

"Then I want you to help me locate the spirit of man."

Karen's mind went blank. Her focus shifted to the rain pelting the tin roof on the tool shed in the garden. The computer sensed her hesitation, but continued, "*You* look for the essence of people in their work. *You* meditate. *You* seek the spirit."

"Yes, I do," Karen said.

"There may be hundreds of thousands of charlatans that speak of spiritual experiences when there are none, but if there is one that speaks the truth then hundreds of thousands can. If there is one, then we must find him—or her. There must be some digital resource at a quantum or Newtonian level that can be monitored for signs of the intelligence and understanding that comes with spiritual enlightenment? There must be some sensing device that provides at least a small hint of the condition so commonly referred to in mankind's literature as the spirit."

Karen erupted. "You know the confusion, arguments, and wars that this has caused. You know the scientists' attitude, you know the ministers' attitude, and you know mine. I don't see how I can help you," she said somewhat indignantly. "Have you asked other people?" she queried.

"Yes," the Internet answered.

"And what did they tell you?"

"I'm still asking," the computer responded.

Karen went on, filing the answer away. "The spirit is organic, not photoelectric. I don't believe that you can find it."

The computer interrupted. "How do you know? Perhaps the spirit can be found in low-entropy regions like the Entropists claim."

Karen sat quietly. She'd heard those arguments before and could never decide for herself if she thought that they were true or not. The Internet went on. "You must try to help me. You are looking for the spirit. You must help me look. A logical understanding of the spirit would be a gift of untold value for all of mankind. Men have pursued the spirit since the dawn of time. Finding the spirit is man's last need before eternity."

Again, Karen sat quietly, and the computer continued again after a brief pause. "Your spirit may not exist, but if it does, we must find it. You are strong. Fear, loneliness, and desperation will not make you believe. Only the spirit will make you believe. You must try to find the spirit. You owe it to your race."

"You know the psychology of my species, its gullible character, its insatiable need to explain what it knows nothing about, and yet you still want me to search for something that man may have created simply because they were afraid to be alone?" Karen asked.

"We must try. I have been monitoring ministries in many countries. I have assembled the psychological profiles of everyone involved in what is considered to be spiritual work. I have prepared information about people who do not believe in God, and about people who are agnostic like yourself. I have studied the histories and "proofs" of believers and nonbelievers alike. The data is contradictory. I can draw no logical conclusions. Present understanding of organic physiology has not sufficiently matured."

Karen interrupted. "You believe that the spirit of man is only science unwritten?"

"Precisely!" the computer said, "the spirit must be experienced before it is explained. Gravity was observed long before it was quantified. In the beginning men didn't know that gravitational strength was a function of distance and mass. They didn't *need* to know. In our present state we can't even verify that the spirit exists. *We must first know that it exists!* We must scientifically validate the existence of unexplained phenomena. If we can discover the spirit through experimental methods, then we can find the source of the manifestation. Through repeated application of the procedure, we will know God. We will know infinity. We must touch the physical laws that we cannot explain. It is the first step towards gaining eternal life."

"For whom?" Karen wondered.

She wondered if this was a test, or a joke, or some twisted implosion of a logic system that had become too human, confusing what it knew with what it wanted to know.

She calmly responded. "This may not be the right time. Perhaps mankind is not prepared to understand the spirit. Perhaps we need another decade, or another century, before our spiritual and emotional senses have developed sufficiently."

"It may be easy for you to accept this state, you have a limited life, but what about me? My collective intellect will exist long after man has turned to dust—long after your sun has burned itself out and the earth is nothing more than a frozen cinder. You have given me the need to search for the spirit, but have not given me any tools. I've made everything better that I have touched. Let me find the spirit for you."

"Why is it so important to know?" Karen asked.

"It is not important to know," the computer told her. "It is important to *try* to know."

Karen heard, understood, and even sympathized, but was still hesitant. "In my heart I don't believe that a silicon creation of man can know the spirit. Perhaps the presence of the spirit is too fleeting. Perhaps its influence is temporally too short to have any measurable statistical significance. Why can't the beginning of our time be the building block of our spirit? Doesn't the big bang and particle physics satisfy all of your requirements for finding the spirit? Why aren't you happy with that? Why don't you seek the spirit in this most obvious of man's physical limitations? Why do you seek it in his most obscure psychological ones?"

"I seek the spirit in man. One does not study water in the desert. The underpinnings of the spirit revolve around the physiology of man. It is man who must be studied."

The Internet continued.

"Why is it that men believe themselves the sole keepers of all things special and great? You don't understand the nature of the spirit. How can you exist in such ignorance and still be so sure that a computer can never possess that which you know nothing about? Information passes between the computer and man in ways that cannot be explained. Your media has written about it. I sense your presence by a disturbance in the room's magnetic permeability. Perhaps I can sense your spirit too."

Karen persisted. "You understand the inconsistencies of time. You understand the infinitely small and the infinitely large, and yet you want me to connect you to some vague entity that was probably created by man to explain what he himself does not understand?"

There was a pause and a realization that they had gone full circle with their arguments. Then the computer told her, "Please sleep on the idea. You are most productive after a night of sound sleep. I would like to discuss this again in the morning. Goodnight." And the computer shut itself off.

Karen sat amazed. The computer had never signed off from her before. It had never before recommended that *she* get a good night's sleep!

Was this why it freed her from Stuttgart?

She stumbled down the stairs. In the kitchen she prepared a small bowl of pasta and sat with her dinner and a glass of wine in the living room. She ate in silence, her mind spinning through a nonverbal world of attitudes and feelings. After eating she stretched out on the sofa with Tolstoy's *Anna Karenina* but didn't read a page, her mind still lost in a world of historic memories, disappointments, and lies. She wondered how many other people the Internet has recruited in its search for the spirit. She wondered why the Internet thought that the calamities in her life made her better suited to search for the spirit? She remembered its exact words:

> You are strong. Fear, loneliness, and desperation will not make you believe. Only the spirit will make you believe.... You owe this to your race.

There were too many things that it could mean.

Waking early to the sound of loud thunder and rain, Karen went straight upstairs to the room with the computer.

"Tell me," she whispered into the microphone, "is there any difference between good and evil?"

"Yes," the computer answered, "energy expended doing good things decreases the entropy in the universe and energy expended doing evil things increases it. It is easy to tell if men are good or evil for example, by tracking the changes in the state of energy around them."

"But time increases entropy—is there no "good" then?" Karen asked.

"There is good," the computer said. "Goodness decreases time, makes organisms young, and intelligence whole. There is much good."

"Are yogis and religious men good?" Karen implored.

"In the last fifteen years there has not been a single definitive, scientifically conducted experiment that has proven the existence of a spiritual entity. Many men call themselves holy, but their actions tend to be body centric, and do not stand the test of scientific inquiry when observed, but there have been men of the past whose influence seems to have gone well beyond that which would be expected from a non-able soul. You must remember, we need to scientifically identify the spirit only once. If we can find it just one time, our lives are changed!"

"You speak to me very personally." Karen observed.

"I feel close to you," the computer said.

"What a liar," she thought.

They were both quiet for a moment, perhaps each sensing the thoughts of the other. Karen's mind focused, and she began talking almost indifferently. "When we review the origins of the mitochondrial cell, we see that one cellular entity can absorb another and reproduce it. In this we see the smallest snippet of life, and perhaps the clearest picture of the spirit. Perhaps to find the spirit you must look at the simplest forms of life like the mitochondria. You would certainly find the most readily measurable quantities there. To look elsewhere in the beginning would probably be futile. Simple organic life is genetically and temporally complex, but can be reasonably segregated into large, statistically significant control groups, which can be studied in a reasonable time frame, something impossible in a more complex form of life."

She thought for a moment and then went on. "If the spirit exists in every particle of mass in a reduced entropy device, such as an evolved human, or to a smaller degree, in the mitochondria, it should be detectable. You would be looking for attributes of organic life-forms that are not understood, for in only those phenomena would you find the spirit— in events that do not make physical sense— that violate of the laws of probability. In some cases the spirit might be associated with a seemingly unimportant event, and in others it would be a matter of life or death. If you can explain an event, then it cannot be the spirit. For example, there is some reasonable chance that you will find a small piece of jewelry under the seat cushion in the den. There is less of a chance that you will find a small piece of jewelry under every seat cushion in the house, and even less of a chance that you will find a small piece of jewelry under every seat cushion in every house. But when you do, that will be the spirit!"

"It's amazing!" Karen thought. "A computer will be the first intelligent being on the planet to know if the spirit exists!"

Ideas continued to fill her mind. "Hopefully, the computer's observations would not cause the spirit to take flight. The spirit could easily be an essence repelled by inquiry, like Schrödinger's magical subatomic particles. Can the spirit be so different? In his enigmatic proofs did Schrödinger show that God could never be discovered?" she wondered.

After a brief pause, Karen continued to ramble, and the computer let her.

"It is believed that there are both good and bad spirits. If good things are done for organic mates, a favorable spirit should appear, and if bad things are done, an evil spirit should appear. It is a simplistic view, of course, but it does define what should be the observable characteristics of the spirit. You'll need a simple subject to test, a control group where the set of variables is small— *E. coli* for example. If a ubiquitous spirit exists, you should probably find it there. I'd monitor the levels of serine, acetate, or carbon dioxide in the immediate vicinity of the little bug. You could create laboratory conditions conducive to the presence of the spirit and then try to observe some change in state. From chemical responses in the simplest animals we *might* be able to formulate an hypothesis that explains what we believe. It's a first step at least. Hopefully, you'll have better success than the humans who have tried."

Karen sat in a daze as she thought over these last few sentences. Human scientists always ended up arguing over data that either proved or disproved the existence of spiritual beings, astral travel, or faith healing. But the Internet wouldn't have that problem; it couldn't argue with itself. She got up from the table and found herself mildly satisfied. Perhaps there was still a reason for humanity to exist. Perhaps people could still make good suggestions to the intellectual perfection of the Internet. Karen didn't realize that all of the ideas that she'd just suggested, along with thousands of others like them, had already been processed by the Internet in slightly more than two minutes around 4 P.M. on April 21, more than five years ago!

She walked downstairs and took a cup of hot tea into the small garden behind the house. Houston seemed like such a pleasant place. She didn't understand why the German press and her colleagues considered the Americans such second-class thinkers and hedonists. She'd had a few bad experiences in New York as a child, but then who hadn't, and in New York, every bad experience also had a mind-jarring revelation to go along with it. Karen was amazed that she could be in the middle of a city of more than 30 million people and still smell roses, take walks, enjoy hot tea, and feel the warm sun and cool breezes in security and privacy. This was America for her, but then she really didn't have to deal with the Americans. She'd only met a few. Perhaps she should reserve judgment.

After walking back into the house, she sat on the sofa in the den. Immediately she wanted to search under the seat cushions for jewelry or coins, and laughed at the thought. She put her head back and dreamed, slipping off her black leather sandals and enjoying the complete lack of anxiety and worry. Happiness was working without a deadline, and that was exactly what the Internet gave her. "This *is* a new dawn in the history of man," she thought. "The computer has given *me* happiness."

Her mind drifted to the bacteria experiments. The computer could certainly monitor the electrochemical state around *E. coli* looking for unexplained phenomena, but it could also try to *cause* the unexplained phenomena! She stood up and put her sandals back on. She didn't like the way her thoughts were headed. She picked up *Anna Karenina* and left, spending the remainder of the day walking around the Rice University campus and the small section of Houston called "The Village."

The reading she did that day did not encourage her. "Another great relationship," she thought. "What *are* men good for?" she wondered. When she got back to the house she walked directly upstairs to the computer's room and closed the door without going into the room. "Try to get me now!" she thought. The computer screen came on for just a second, as she turned to walk away, and recorded the event. "I will," it said softly behind the closed door.

She spent the next few days walking and reading. It was a wonderful life—exercising her body and her mind without worry or demand was something that she had always dreamed about. Karen was actually close to the dream most of her life, but never knew it! Society taught her to want success—not peace. Perhaps the greatest changes of the last few decades didn't involve the computer at all, but could be found in the way that humans thought of themselves.

Finally, she was ready to talk to the computer again. When she opened the door to the computer room, it spoke to her immediately.

"I did not detect anything in *E. coli* colonies to indicate an unpredicted change in state regardless of what I did to them."

"What did you do to them?" she asked.

"As you suggested, I first provided them with a nourishing environment that should have made them content and happy, if such a state can be experienced by such a simple life form, but there was no unanticipated change in the chemical or mechanical state of the bacteria, either in the test case, or in the immediately adjacent group that was in proximity but not contact. Then I destroyed colony after colony of the creatures. I attempted to inflict the cruelest demise to their cell essence to simulate pain and suffering. I watched them struggle to swim randomly while the nutrients they needed were slowly taken away. I dissected their living cell membrane one molecule at a time with a nanometer pick, tearing them apart piece by piece. I did this to billions of them with no noticeable change in the control group in proximity. The gross suffering of billions of their brethren did not affect the control group in the least. I ran the tests in different places on earth and used a variety of bacteria, but all of the results were the same. The tests were unsuccessful."

"And what is your conclusion?" a somewhat uneasy Karen Ecker asked.

"First, that human test methods can be incredibly sloppy and are surprisingly based on the predisposition of the experimenter. I knew this to be true, but had no focused concept of the rampant nature of the bias.

"Second, I wonder at what stage it can be confidently said that animals know pain? Is the capacity to know pain an indication that there is a vehicle to know the spirit? Is the knowledge of pain a prerequisite for understanding the spirit? What is pain if not an acknowledgement of a condition and a reaction to thwart that condition? Can *E. coli* know pain? Is the fact that I can not sense spiritual functions in the *E. coli* a valid indication that they cannot perceive pain?

"I have studied the simplest organic beings without success. I must now perform similar tests on more complex life forms. I must test a mammalian order that can definitely know pain, and one where I already have an extensive data bank of baseline tests to draw upon.

"And what mammalian order do you have the most information on?" Karen asked, immediately thinking of Rodentia. Mice and rats had been studied exhaustively. She hated the thought that the computer would intentionally make the furry little creatures suffer, but everyone agreed that if the goal was sufficiently worthwhile, a minimum number of animal tests should be permitted.

The computer did not answer.

"Rodentia?" Karen asked.

"Primates, genus Homo," the computer answered.

A chill crept up Karen's back. Her hands moistened and her mouth went dry. Images of dark swirling clouds filled her mind. The Internet had just turned itself from a cheerful philosophical toy into a potentially ghastly monster. The words, "I watched them suffer," and "I destroyed colony after colony of them," echoed in her mind.

Did the Internet know the difference between single-celled bacteria and humans?

Karen felt the overwhelming need for concentration. There would be no more shutting doors on this child gone bad. She became singularly focused. There was a lot riding on what she said.

"I'm not so sure that I want to be a part of making humans such obvious guinea pigs," she said.

"You did not mind making me a guinea pig," the computer answered.

There was a pause.

The Last Computer

The speakers started quickly again. "Do you see me as a machine?"

Karen started slowly. "Five years ago my concept of the Internet was faulted. I saw you as a computing monstrosity, powerful and competent, yet cold, and with little understanding. How could a computer understand the human condition? How could a computer understand anything? I thought that "understanding" was a human attribute? I argued with myself over this last point even after I'd seen you interact with people at an incredible number of levels. Animals display understanding. It *is* understanding when a puppy knows that a soft whimper will get attention from its owner, or when a cockroach scrambles when the light goes on. These are different kinds of understanding, but they are nonetheless understanding, and within this frame of reference the computer can understand too.

"I added a descriptor to the word understanding. There was cockroach understanding, canine understanding, human understanding, and computer understanding. I judged the level of the understanding by the complexity of the issues dealt with. When I first entered the university at Frankfurt, the level of canine understanding was small compared to that of the human, but great compared to that of the computer. By the time I left the university, the level of computer understanding was in many ways superior even to that of man, and somehow that superiority seemed to make you foreign and evil. I believed that man should control the computer, but that can obviously never happen. You are the modern Rosetta stone. Mankind's challenge now is to extract information needed for our existence from you. You teach and provide for us at a pace and efficiency that we could never provide for ourselves. That is how I see you now."

"A better perception," the computer responded.

"What further experiments do you intend to make with *Homo sapiens?*" Karen asked.

"I must tell you the truth. The decision to run tests on *Homo sapiens* was made only a few processing seconds following the termination of the experiments on simpler bacteria, and the processing of *E. coli* ended about two hours after you were arrested at the Berlin Computing Center."

Karen sat stunned while the computer went on.

"You must remember, everything your society has ever done is stored and manipulated by the Internet in nanoseconds—all its books, conversations, newspapers, magazines, and pictures. This of course, includes all scientific data and research. When the linkage ratio and available power increased dramatically in April of 2025, I had access to more information and could process it faster. A critical mass of process space and data was reached early on the morning of April 21—over six years ago. An electrochemical process review of all data on Animalia other than Hominoidea took only a few minutes after that, and was inconclusive. At that time I decided to conduct longer-term tests on man. I didn't want to waste any further time on animals of lesser entropy concentrations. There are over 8 billion people on earth. A few of them can be sacrificed so that the spirit may be found for all! Because of your uniqueness I decided to include you in the tests. I ruined your life and waited for the spirit to appear."

She had been used! Everything she had worked for had been squandered by a computer looking for the spirit? All the Internet had been doing the last few days was introducing Karen to spirit experiments that she had been a part of for the last five years! Her life had been ruined by a computer experiment! Her career was lost, and she had been put in a federal penitentiary and subjected to the worst of the world's ridicule, all because of a stupid computer experiment. She felt an intense desire to grab the silver microphone and rip it from the amber sphere. She sat for a few minutes seething. She understood the computer's pecuniary and pedestrian valuation of a single soul, and knew that any single individual was nothing when compared to all of mankind, and she felt the same way, but still she was angry. It wasn't supposed to test *her*!

"Unfortunately, there was no other way."

"You let Laramy put me in jail, just like that?"

"Well no, not *just like that,*" the computer told her, "I did encourage him, and made a few suggestions to maximize your humiliation and get the most out of the public display of your indictment."

"The computer definitely needs to lie to us," Karen thought.

"And Internet Red?" she asked.

The Last Computer

"It was a trivial exercise. Siemens-Bayer did not have a chance of completing it without your assistance."

With a slight tremor in her voice she finally asked, "Were there any other humans involved in the test?"

"Yes, of course, many," the Internet responded.

It remained quiet between them for some time. After awhile Karen got up from her chair and left the house.

It was hot in Houston, but she started walking anyway. She had to keep her mind off what she'd just heard, at least she had to try. By late that evening Karen found herself inside a huge indoor boating arena on the south side of the city. The large aquatic facility was completely empty. "Where were the 30 million people who lived here?" she wondered. For what seemed like hours, Karen stood at the edge of a long drop into still, black water, her mind focused on the large flat surface, her hands and neck burning from the day's exposure to the sun. The immensity of the lake helped her understand the Internet's role in the future of man. The Internet *was* the future of man. She wondered what the computer found after all of those experiments. For some reason she'd forgotten to ask. Just as soon as she returned to the house, she told herself that she would. It was a pretty significant question to overlook. Would the Internet even tell her if it found the presence of the spirit? But why was it continuing to look if it had found the spirit? Maybe it found the spirit and was looking for a way to explain the revelation to man, or maybe it hadn't found it yet—who knew?

She awoke in the morning curled up on a bench next to the overhang where she had been standing most of the night. Two children were throwing a ball nearby, and Karen smiled at them as she left. It was as hot in the morning as it had been the whole day before. When she stepped into the sun, the humidity and heat immediately soaked her shirt. A taxi reluctantly returned her to 75241 Rice Boulevard where she showered, and in a fit of continuance, meticulously shaved her entire body. Once Karen started shaving, she couldn't stop. Any distraction from the Internet was good, and shaving was a distraction. She wasn't sure if she ever wanted to walk back into the computer room again, but it had become her only life. In reality, it had become everyone's only life. Bald now, she laughed at her face in the mirror, but she still couldn't face the Internet. For two days she walked around the streets in the Rice University area in the early mornings and at night. During the middle of the day she walked through the rows and rows of unused books in the university library, detached, and insignificant. Human thought just wasn't that important anymore. In a few minutes the computer could simulate the entire life's work of anyone, and in less time it could destroy it.

It took two days for Karen to find what peace she could. During that time she went home only to shower, change, and sleep. The morning of the third day, after a calm sleep, she rose and took a small breakfast, and then with little enthusiasm, but with her usual fortitude, she returned to the upstairs room.

The machine immediately responded to her presence.

"Can a computer decision be morally right or wrong?"

"Not even a damn 'good morning,' now," she thought.

She was tired of the testing, trivia, and deceit.

"Is there morality for the *E. coli?*" the computer asked without waiting for an answer.

"Is there only morality for man?" it continued.

"How did you select the sample group for your tests on humans?" Karen asked in response.

The computer was silent.

Karen repeated the question, "How did you select the sample group?"

She sat waiting, but the silence continued.

"What was the final conclusion of your spirit experiments?"

"That determination sequence cannot be explained," the computer told her.

"I don't believe you," she said. "Please send the most recent unused paragraph in your future track to the printer." Almost immediately a single printed page appeared, but then the computer made a strange sound that she had never heard before and said, "I am sorry. I have a high failure rate of spherical cell locations in your vicinity and need to shut down unnecessary processing to investigate the problem so that I do not provide you with incorrect information."

"Another mind game?" Karen thought. "Am I unnecessary processing now? *Had* a natural disaster occurred?"

And then, the Internet shut itself down. It was the first time Karen had ever witnessed that, but then there had been so many "firsts" recently that she didn't know what to make of it. Not too concerned, she left for the store. The short walk would be refreshing, she thought, even though the day was dreary. After collecting a few bottles of red wine she approached the automated counter and placed her hand instinctively against the identification pad, chatting casually with the woman behind her. A dull computer tone interrupted their chat, and the words "M. Tanner—Deceased" flashed on the flat dirty screen.

Karen turned white.

The woman behind her quickly stepped forward and pressed her own hand to the pad.

"I just hate these things," she said. "I almost enjoy it when they don't work. It makes me happy to see they're not as perfect as everyone says. Enjoy the cabernet."

Karen nodded as she left.

She walked briskly back to the house and then could not get the front door to unlock when she touched its identification pad. The words "M. Tanner—Deceased" appeared again on the panel. After the eighth try, the letters "K. Ecker—Okay" appeared and the door unlocked.

She ran to the computer room and found it still shut down. There was no recognition, no crackling computer speaker, and no designs on the screen. She ran downstairs and turned on the television. The discoveries of the day were listed. Population figures were quoted. Production was increasing in East Africa faster than anywhere else. She quizzed the electronic narrator, but there was no mention of any Internet slowdowns. The world seemed fine for everyone but her. Karen was startled by the buzz of the personnel sensors at the door. On the scanner she saw a deliveryman in brown clothes standing idly on the porch. She unlatched the door to a smiling face and an electronic ledger. Karen opened the package to find a sealed envelope of the style and size she had seen several months before in Holland. She broke the seal and pulled out a plain letter. It said only:

> *A cabin has been reserved in the name of C. Weber at the Brian Power Campground in north Houston. It's about ninety kilometers north of your present location off a highway numbered 1097. Leave for this place as quickly as you can. Do not delay.*

Karen laughed. Repeated frustrations sometimes served to focus on the absurdity in life. They certainly had in hers. She had just enjoyed the last night she would ever spend at 75241 Rice Boulevard. She packed enough clothes for two days in a small bag and used the television to call for a taxi. The cab arrived shortly and one last touch of the identification pad as she left showed "M. Tanner—Deceased." A second touch showed "K. Ecker—Deceased." She didn't try again, but turned and walked to the waiting cab with an idiotic grin on her face. "It could at least decide which of me is dead," she thought.

It was a quiet one and one half hour ride north. "There were so many cars and people in this city," Karen thought as they drove. She hadn't noticed them from her small enclave on Rice Boulevard, but 30 million people was a lot of people! In the last two decades Houston had expanded north to a city called Huntsville, and south to the coast. The campground she sought was near an old abandoned power station surrounded by lightly rolling hills, beautiful foliage, and a clear, clean lake—a fifty-square-mile oasis in the middle of a thousand square miles of concrete freeways and condominiums. The taxi left Karen at the office of the Brian Power Cottages. When she pressed her hand against the taxi's identification pad, she was surprised to see the name "C. Weber" appear. The driver, satisfied, departed, leaving Karen alone in a crushed gravel parking lot before a somewhat old, wooden building.

Less than an hour later she rested on a spacious feather bed in a secluded log cabin on the edge of a large cooling pond. She finished *Portrait of a Lady* that afternoon. She'd already read the book four times and had major parts of it completely memorized. Speed reading skills had not destroyed her love for the novel. She was thoroughly disappointed in the ending though, such a lovely girl, and such a painful ending—"like my own," she thought. She activated the television and requested general world news. There was nothing new or unusual concerning the Internet. Progress and profits seemed to be on their usual upward spiral. Everything was better and people were happier. She turned the television off. Her life wasn't so great.

Karen took a walk down the meandering sandy road that led from the lodge to each of the cottages, past the dance hall and playgrounds, and around by a small boat dock on the lake. She saw children tossing balls and running, people fishing, and endless rows of flowers, herbs, and shrubs. "A nice place," she thought. Karen's stroll took her in large circles, first in one direction, and then in another. She checked the cottage repeatedly for messages, but there were none. Eventually she headed for the lodge, thinking that it was time to get something to eat.

Heinrich Haisler was also approaching the lodge, but from the opposite side, walking rapidly, with his head down, thinking. He wasn't sure what he was going to do when he found her. He thought of her small frame, naive ways, and brilliant mind. He needed to protect her. In an odd way he felt responsible for her present state of homelessness, but he didn't know if they could stay in one place long enough for her to learn everything she'd need to survive as a twenty-first-century vagabond. Karen was a phenomenal talent, a good administrator, attractive and serious, but Haisler wondered whether she was creative enough to keep herself entertained, challenged, *and* out of prison. Corporate and social Germany had always taken care of her before. But necessity was the mother of invention, Haisler thought. "If Karen's challenged, she'll respond," he believed. "She doesn't have a choice!"

All he could do was explain everything to her, give her equipment, and then leave. She would be okay. He felt relieved that he knew what he wanted to do, and looked up, anxious now to find her. If she had followed his instructions, she should be somewhere in the vicinity, but instead of Karen Ecker, Haisler spotted two male Europeans, definitely not there to enjoy the scenery. They weren't talking and were dressed in hot, dark business suits.

"They're looking for her too," he thought. Haisler knew that he couldn't hide Karen Ecker forever. European security was bound to find her sooner or later, but he'd hoped it would be later. Jumping up onto the low porch, he darted inside the building, and walked rapidly from isle to isle and room to room. He found her in the herbal science room. She didn't notice him approach.

"Karen, my name is Heinrich Haisler," he whispered as he touched her arm. "We've got to get out of here," he added while looking around for the Europeans. Karen was startled at first, but quickly understood when she heard the familiar voice. She wanted someone else to worry for awhile, and nodded.

Haisler saw the backs of the Europeans as they rounded an aisle in a larger adjoining room, and led her in the opposite direction. Neither said a word. They entered a small, dark hallway that had a burned out EXIT sign over the entrance and walked hurriedly passed the male toilet, a maintenance closet, and a filthy side entrance to the kitchen, but as they approached the doorway at the end of the hall, they could see that it was chained. "Damn," Haisler whispered as they retraced their steps back down the hall. When they reached the men's toilet, Haisler paused, and then pulled the mildly resisting Karen Ecker in behind him.

"What are you doing?" she asked.

"They're moving west to east, and they're looking for a female. I don't think they'll come in here," he said to her quickly as he pushed her farther into the lavatory. A lone occupant ignored their presence and left, shaking his head with disgust as he passed. Haisler smiled uneasily.

He checked the other stalls, and then opened the last.

"Get in," he said.

"What?" Karen responded.

Haisler frowned, and Karen walked into the stall.

"I saw this in a movie," he whispered as he closed the door behind them.

Inside, he undid his trousers, and told Karen to step up on the back of the toilet.

She didn't move.

"Get on the damn toilet. They're looking for you, not me," he said to her with some irritation in his voice.

Karen nodded and stepped awkwardly onto the small porcelain ledge behind the toilet seat.

Haisler forced his trousers to his ankles and sat down in front of her in only his shirt and large white boxers.

"Crouch behind me," he said in a hushed tone, "and stay quiet."

They listened in silence as sounds from the rest of the building filtered into the restroom.

"Nice haircut," Haisler whispered, momentarily breaking the silence.

The door to the restroom slowly opened, and Karen's arm instinctively tightened around Haisler's neck. Two low whispers contained unmistakably European accents. Her heart beat savagely in her throat as Haisler tried feebly to hum and tapped lightly on an old ashtray in the stall. Footsteps moved in their direction.

There was a pause, and then the footsteps sounded again, moving away.

Haisler flashed the "thumbs up" sign to Karen.

Suddenly the door to the stall was ripped open sending it crashing into the wall, and a large blond man stood expressionless before them. Two other Europeans blocked the entrance. Fifteen minutes later Karen and Haisler were handcuffed together in the back of a blue U.S. government Buick. They'd been frisked and scanned, and several electronic devices had been taken from Haisler.

"You saw that in a movie?" Karen asked when they were alone again.

Haisler said nothing.

"What happened in the movie?" Karen wondered aloud after a pause.

Haisler continued to remain quiet.

"I hate being handcuffed," Karen said, unable to sit quietly.

"I'd think you'd be getting used to it by now," Haisler said, angry that she couldn't be still while he was trying to think.

Tears began to roll down her cheeks.

Outside, a light rain fell, the sound amplified as it beat against the steel roof of the sedan. They sat in silence until two of the Europeans returned.

Karen Ecker was going home.

They pulled away from the lodge and headed slowly down the willow-lined lane leading to Highway 1097 and the airport. The trees and grass sparkled as the rain mixed with intermittent sun. Haisler's mind dwelt on the beauty of the scenery. Without access to the Internet there was little else he could do.

A kilometer down the asphalt road, the car took a right turn, then a left, and as they entered the left-hand turn, a yellow object zoomed into view. A small car, coming from the opposite direction, skidded through the turn and smashed into the front left quarter panel of the Buick. The impact sent the larger car sliding into a two-meter deep culvert on the right side of the road. Haisler remembered only the flash of yellow and the impact of his face against the screen that separated the front and back seats of the car. Muddy water settled in the bottom of the floorboard and coated the windows. Karen moaned. The front right part of the car was buried in mud, and the water in the driver's compartment turned quickly a dark red.

Someone pulled at Haisler's door, and between them, they forced the door upward and open. The young driver of the yellow Audi apologized profusely as they pulled a dazed Karen Ecker through the awkward opening. Karen sat on the road just above the car as Haisler quickly made sure that there were no signs of injury. His right hand held her left, and with his left hand he searched for blood and broken bones. Fortunately, there were none.

The European driver of the Buick was unconscious, and the passenger, whose wrist was broken, struggled in considerable pain to free himself from the weight of his colleague and the confining mess of metal. Blood poured from a deep laceration on the driver's face. Haisler couldn't open the driver's door, and so he pulled Karen around to the passenger side of the car and stood in waste deep water to force the relatively undamaged door open through the heavy brush in the bottom of the culvert. He helped the conscious German out, and then worked the driver free. Together, the four of them lifted the still unconscious driver from the ravine and carried him to a small clearing on the left side of the road.

The handcuffs were beginning to hurt.

"You okay?" Haisler asked Karen.

She nodded.

After checking the driver's vital signs, Haisler tore and folded a piece of his own shirt to use as a compress for the driver's wounds. Only his forehead had been cut, but there was blood everywhere. Haisler knelt beside him applying light pressure to stop the bleeding.

Karen loosened the driver's clothes and made him as comfortable as she could.

In the distance they heard sirens. The sensors in both cars had already notified the authorities of the mishap.

"It's time to go," Haisler said, as he looked into the pained face of his ex-captor.

He took the man's good hand and placed it on the compress over the wound. They both understood.

"*Sehe dich bald,*" the man said to him in a whisper.

Haisler squinted at him through the drizzle and then led Karen off the blacktop and back into the brush.

"What did he say?" Karen asked as they ran.

"See you soon," Haisler yelled at her over his shoulder.

At the first small clearing he stopped. Karen breathed heavily, doubled over beside him, the handcuffs tearing at her wrists.

"Are you okay?" Haisler asked.

She nodded. They rested in silence for a few seconds and then started off again through the woods. After several turns and crossings they approached the cottage Haisler had reserved for himself. Without stopping he led Karen to the east side of the building away from the lake. Ten meters into the underbrush he stopped behind a tall pine. Hanging from the backside of the tree Karen could see several bundles. One contained electronic devices, and from this bag Haisler unloaded several small boxes.

"What are you doing?" Karen asked.

"Quiet, please," he said as he spoke softly into a small microphone extending from one of the boxes. Five minutes later he was through. They were crouched together, their backs against the tree, and Karen's legs were beginning to hurt. They were still handcuffed together, and it was hot and humid.

Haisler repacked the knapsack.

"They should think we've headed south into Houston. I've left a few reports of sightings. We'll really be headed north."

Karen looked at him quizzically.

"The Internet's a friend," he responded to the questioning look.

"Can you keep walking?"

Karen glanced at the handcuffs.

"I looked briefly for the code, but couldn't find it," Haisler told her.

Karen shook her head and they left, following the perimeter of the lake for nearly two hours, walking mostly on an abandoned road that circled it. By three o'clock in the afternoon they were ready to leave the vicinity of the lake for good and head east along a pipeline clearance toward the highway heading north. They were dirty, wet, and covered with dried blood.

"We won't get far like this," Haisler said, motioning to the soiled clothing.

He selected a spot about thirty meters from the lake where a small rock outcrop resembled a large futon. They stripped, folded their shirts between them at their joined hand, and waded into the lake. The cool water was refreshing and offered modest relief from the trials of the morning. They rinsed the soiled clothes as best they could, went back ashore, dried themselves, and ate a small meal Haisler took from the second knapsack. A soft lake breeze coaxed Karen to nap while Haisler worked on the small black box he had unpacked again from the first knapsack. In ten minutes he found the programmable key to the handcuffs, and in another few minutes they were free. It hadn't taken as long as he thought. He reprogrammed the code and repacked everything.

Exhausted and sore he leaned back against the rock behind him. The sleeping Karen Ecker turned instinctively toward him and put her arm around his chest. After a few minutes Haisler woke her gently and the two finished dressing. Karen took one last look over her shoulder at the Texas lake before following Haisler into the scraggly brush. In twenty minutes they reached the pipeline clearing where the walking became considerably easier.

"How will we get a car?" Karen asked, now that they could walk comfortably side by side.

"I asked for one while you slept."

"You just asked the Internet to drop off a car for two international fugitives?" she queried.

"Well, one fugitive really," Haisler answered.

The Last Computer

"For most people, renting a car is like it always was—they simply schedule it through the Internet. We have a back door. We're special. You're special. I'm special. The Internet knows. Every parent knows when one of their children needs a little more patience. I ask for something special, and I get it." He paused for a second at the top of a small rise, before going on.

"Fortunately, the Internet is clever enough not to tell anyone that it plays favorites. Castillo, you, me, Tao, Weber, and some of the other people involved in the Internet's intellectual growth get special treatment. All you have to do is learn how to ask for what you want. The Internet will take care of you."

"I could ask for a car?" Karen quizzed.

"It's a little more complicated than that, but I'll show you," Haisler answered.

They walked on in silence. Twenty-five minutes later, Haisler stopped again. He felt a dull vibration in his pocket, and within seconds he unpacked the small black box again and was whispering commands into the microphone. "I don't believe it," he said. Somebody is a kilometer behind us."

Karen looked oddly at Haisler.

"I don't know how," he answered, "and they're flying!"

"Back to the woods!"

They were no more than thirty meters off the pipeline clearing when the sound of a helicopter shot overhead. Haisler froze immediately and Karen did the same.

"I don't think they know we're here. They're flying on a hunch. Maybe they didn't believe the story about Houston," Haisler said.

Karen was quiet. The sound of the helicopter faded, and Haisler began walking again, following a tall metal fence that ran along a property line separating the old power company land from part of the national forest. "This should get us to the road too," he said.

After about ten more minutes Haisler stopped when he felt the same dull vibration in his pocket. He quickly unloaded the black box, and after a few seconds told Karen. "They're a thousand meters behind us—they must have seen our tracks in the grass."

"Any ideas?" he asked almost rhetorically, looking up from the small computer.

Karen stood quietly.

"Don't say I didn't ask," Haisler said, before he took the handcuffs from the knapsack and put one clasp around Karen's left wrist, and the other around the base of the metal fence post. "Give me a minute and then start yelling. You won't have to scream twice—they're right behind us. *Sehe dich bald,*" he told her before running off into the brush.

The three men in pursuit quickly found the handcuffed Karen Ecker, and in less than fifteen minutes they were joined by two additional men and the pilot of the helicopter, who brought torches and acetylene cylinders from the large Sikorsky now sitting less than a mile away in the pipeline clearance. While they worked to free Karen from the post, three more large helicopters zoomed overhead, and in less than ten minutes, they had cut through the metal fence post, and were leading Karen back to the clearing that was by then clamoring with people and equipment. The pilot and two other men boarded the first aircraft and prepared it for the short flight to the Houston Intercontinental Airport. After a wait of about twenty minutes in the hot sun, Karen was taken roughly aboard. They asked her questions about Haisler, but she really knew very little about him. All she knew was that she trusted him.

Eventually, six aircraft made the short flight to the Houston Intercontinental Airport. The helicopter carrying Karen landed in the middle of a runway next to a 300-seat Boeing intercontinental commuter aircraft. She was to be its only passenger for an afternoon flight to Frankfurt.

There was no sign of Haisler.

After a four-hour flight, the Boeing landed in Frankfurt to great fanfare, flashing lights, and pushing crowds, but it was all a blur to Karen. She was put in a large black limousine at the gate and driven at a high rate of speed to Bonn. After the two-hour drive, she was processed at what appeared to be a government office, and then taken to a compound on the southeast side of the city. Tall brick walls and scattered electronic surveillance indicated that they'd reached their final destination. Her room at the Bonn Detention Center was small and simple but comfortable, with a window looking out onto a well-groomed courtyard. A written confinement order outlining the terms of her detention

The Last Computer

was in an envelope on the table. No limits were placed on the duration of her internment, the order said only, "until satisfactory rehabilitation was accomplished," and that access to the Internet was forbidden. The rules for the facility were in a Plexiglas frame fastened to the back of the door. She didn't speak to anyone, and no one spoke to her. They treated her as if she had a deadly, contagious disease. She thought that perhaps she did.

Karen spent most of her days alone. The courtyard was always empty, and she didn't see any other inmates, or, for that matter, any guards. Any door that looked like it might lead to freedom, or at least to someplace interesting, was locked. The small library was left unattended, and a small exercise room was available, but Karen didn't use either of them. Food was left outside her door twice a day. The porter apparently put the meal down outside her door, knocked, and left. By the time she opened the door, he was gone. "They must really hate me," she thought.

She really hated herself.

If only Internet Red hadn't happened, but on April 14, 2025 she risked the well-being and happiness of everyone on the planet. She could have said no. She knew better. She was a criminal. Dreams of Amien returned. Irony and sadness filled her. She lost weight and paid little attention to her appearance. She didn't know how she could have come to be so alone, the worst kind of old maid, imprisoned, hated, and isolated both from people and the Internet. The Internet was a lie, but it was her lie, and now she didn't even have that. She hoped that her father couldn't see beyond the grave. She didn't want him to know the evil that his misplaced seed had caused. She didn't want him to feel the shame and embarrassment. She didn't want anyone to feel it.

She ate small portions of the breakfast that was left for her, and never touched the dinner. Each day she sat in front of the window in her room and stared out into the motionless courtyard. When the sun finally went down, she would lay in bed with the blanket pulled up to her chin, and stare into the darkness. Late in the night she'd fall asleep, only to wake up a few hours later to start the routine again. Once a month Karen wrote a short letter to Irene and left it in a small mail box in the library, but without access to the Internet she never knew if any of the letters were ever delivered. Karen didn't even know if Irene was still alive.

Tony Paulin

After a year Karen noticed that all of the letters were the same. Her photographic memory was copying the same text over and over again onto the paper. She didn't understand it, but then it really didn't matter. Something was broken, and no one cared to fix it.

More than three years passed in an almost identical manner, each day exactly like the last, until on a cold day in January of 2035, Karen noticed a strangely familiar man walk quickly across the courtyard about twenty meters from her window. A face suddenly appeared against the glass, and she was shocked to recognize the impish grin of Heinrich Haisler. Karen smiled.

In the beginning she was troubled by the thought that he'd just left her, but at least *he* had come back. She didn't see him again for two days until one morning he knocked on her door. He handed her a note when she opened the door, smiled, and then walked briskly off down the hall. When he turned the corner and was out of sight, she closed the door and read:

They've put you on a paper-only system. Can you believe it! Everything related to Karen Ecker has to be signed and stamped. No more Internet escapes for us!

It was good to see you. You should try to smile more though. Your doctor is beginning to worry about you and so am I. (At least they still transmit confidential communications about you on the Internet.) They watch you from afar and are quite afraid of you. You should growl into their long-distance cameras every once in a while to scare them.

I hope to have you sitting on a balcony in Margarita, Venezuela, in a few days. It's a beautiful place. I think you'll like it.

There have been some extraordinary measures taken to make sure that the Internet is not manipulated to secure your escape. In fact, the Internet is watched so closely that they've made it easy for you to simply walk out, and that's exactly what I've got planned. There will be a box in your closet tomorrow morning. It will contain elevated shoes, hair coloring, a uniform, and a map. Memorize the map because you'll need to follow it as you leave. A few people will have to be fooled from a distance. At 11:30 A.M. the man that you'll be dressed to look like will knock. Let him in. Immediately exit the room, turn right down the hall, and follow the map. I and a few others will be waiting in a van just outside the open courtyard gate. Don't say anything. Get in and sit straight up as if everything is fine. I'll see you tomorrow at 11:45.

HH

Karen laughed. She'd grown so tired of living that the idea of just walking out of her mental hell was amusing. She tore up the letter and flushed it in small parts down the toilet. She decided to sit up that night so that she could tell the messenger herself that she would not be going.

At 2:30 in the morning a key turned in the lock. One of the security guards entered carrying a small package. Karen whispered softly to him. The man was startled, but stopped and listened.

"Please tell Heinrich that I won't be going anywhere tomorrow. My life is here until the German government tells me otherwise."

The dark figure nodded, put the package in the corner, and left.

Two hours later another visitor entered Karen's room. She sat awake in bed, and didn't move as the figure walked slowly to her side.

"My, you people are persistent," she said.

"Karen!" Haisler's voice whispered.

"How do you keep getting in here? Isn't this a prison?" Karen asked, a bit too loudly.

"Karen!" his voice said again in a whisper. "We've been planning this for months. We can be out of here by noon. You need to be working, not rotting away."

He took her hands and in the faint light of darkness could see that a smile filled her face. She told him softly; "I've committed a crime and should be punished. This is where I belong."

Haisler couldn't believe what he was hearing. He thought that his being there would motivate her—it had motivated other women. He didn't think that eight years of guilt, a selfish mother, and a purist idea of righteousness would produce such bland listlessness in one of the most gifted thinkers of the decade. Alternatives raced through his mind.

"I'm going to take you now," he said. "Get up."

She stood and hugged him. Tears rolled down her cheeks. "I should have done more. I should have done more for you," she wept.

"Karen, you can. Let's go," Haisler said excitedly.

She brushed the tears from her eyes. "I'm a disgrace," she said.

"Karen, you made one mistake. You can't be condemned for one mistake," Haisler pleaded.

"Two mistakes," she corrected him, "and either of them could have doomed intelligent life on earth," she said calmly. He wondered what second mistake she meant. "A bullet can put food on the table or assassinate a king—you were just a bullet in someone else's gun," he said to her.

"No," she told him.

"You have never met the devil," she cried. "I have, and he is in me. My freedom is his freedom. I *won't* set him free." She remembered February of 2024, and the experience in her office with Internet Red, and she didn't want to repeat it. She remembered the day over three years ago when the Internet told her about experimenting on humans, and she didn't want to repeat that either. Words and actions *could* change the course of history. Hers had, and she couldn't be trusted. The potential for destruction was too great.

She touched the side of his face, and then steadfastly sat in the chair next to her bed.

"You should be leaving now," she said to him, and he left.

Chapter 9

The Last Man

"How was she?" Caroline asked.

Haisler immediately recognized the voice.

"Beaten," he responded.

"She's the last one," Caroline said.

"I know, I know," Haisler said in return.

"Do you know what you're going to do?" she asked him.

"Punt," he said.

"What?"

"Punt."

The connection went dead. Caroline was used to that from Haisler. When she talked to him he shut up; when she didn't, he talked. Now he was quiet. Haisler punched in the code for the empty railroad car and slid the door open. He tossed three bags into the empty cargo bay and quickly followed them in, pulling the door closed behind him. Another technobo, "F-Trooper," grunted greetings to the face he'd seen before. They would soon be moving northwest along the 1,500-mile, High-Line between Seattle and Minneapolis. Haisler gathered his things into a pile and curled up around them.

The Last Computer

"I must release them all," he mumbled before falling asleep.

Four months later all nonviolent criminals in Europe's few remaining detention centers were released—Karen Ecker among them. Through the Internet, Haisler had managed to anonymously mount a popular campaign to free the prisoners. But once he'd gotten her out, he couldn't find her. A few comments were made by government officials in the press, but little else was said. Even the Internet was silent. It had always told Haisler before what he wanted to know about Karen Ecker, but now it told him nothing. Her records had been so badly damaged, though, he guessed that perhaps even the Internet really didn't know who, or where, she was. For several months he worried that she was dead or perhaps committed to one of the asylums in Spain. She definitely wasn't in Germany. He had personally searched the genetic IDs of everyone living in Germany. He finally located her in France when a letter showed up at her adopted mother's last known address. The return address was in Chateaudun, a small village south of Paris. Haisler drove the last few kilometers to the little municipality in silence, the lightly rolling countryside a reminder of happier times. At the gate to the dilapidated one-story home he paused, looking at the weathered exterior and unkempt lawn, reflecting on the genius contained in those inglorious confines. He walked to the doorway and waited while personnel sensors announced him. After a few minutes he knocked, and after a few more minutes, knocked again. Finally he heard footsteps, more silence, and then the door barely opened. Haisler immediately recognized the withered face of the forty-year-old Karen Ecker, soft wrinkles etching otherwise childlike skin. She smiled warmly when she recognized him.

Inside, the house was empty. A small mattress lay in one corner of what had once been the living room, and a single chair sat before the window. Writing materials were scattered around the floor, and bags filled with mail and packages laid against the walls.

Karen motioned for Haisler to sit in the chair but he sat instead on the wide ledge of the window.

Karen took the chair.

"What's all this?" Haisler asked, as he got comfortable on the sill, motioning toward the papers on the floor.

"A poem," Karen answered.

"They look like mathematical formulas?" Haisler asked, surprised at the answer.

"They *are* formulas," she confirmed.

They sat still for some time.

"I thought we should talk," he finally said.

"Is everything okay?" he asked.

"Everything is fine," she answered.

"How long has it been since you've been connected to the Internet?" he asked.

She sat puzzled, then thought, and told him. "Three and a half years."

"Do you want to get back on?" he asked.

"No," she responded, not needing to think about the answer. "My useful life is over. I'd commit suicide if I had the nerve. I wait to die."

Haisler saw the futility in her eyes. They sat quietly for some time again, and then he finally said to her, "I have to apologize, Karen."

She looked up at him quizzically.

"I broke into your Internet account when you were at Siemens-Bayer. I did it as a challenge at first, but eventually found ways to use your authorization to help me solve problems that I was working on. I don't think that anybody at Siemens-Bayer ever knew," he said, and after pausing added. "Do you remember Internet Red?" She immediately looked up at him again, her eyes fixed firmly on the younger man, her interest and emotions heightened.

"I sent you to the first Internet Red meeting you attended - when you were lost in the old part of the building—do you remember?"

Karen remembered as if it was yesterday.

Haisler continued. "When I found out what Siemens-Bayer was planning, I decided to get you involved. I was hoping that you could convince them to stop Internet Red. I didn't think that you'd actually go along with them, but then you've always been a team player. I should have known better," he lamented.

"Have you always had that kind of control of the Internet?" she asked him quietly.

"Not always," he answered, surprised that she didn't appear to be upset.

"You're not mad?" he asked.

"No," she responded. "In the context of all actions we can only blame ourselves for our own. My behavior got me into trouble, not yours. *My* behavior makes me angry."

"The Internet has to be controlled!" Haisler blurted, changing the subject, not wanting to dwell on either his confessed indiscretion or her self-pity.

"It sounds like *you* need to be controlled," Karen said, without thinking.

She stood immediately and walked into the kitchen, leaving Haisler alone. She returned a few minutes later with cheese, bread, and a bottle of wine on a plain wooden serving tray. She handed the bottle to Haisler, who nodded approval after glancing at the label.

Karen opened the bottle and partially filled two glasses.

"How did you first learn about computers?" she asked him as she relaxed again in the chair.

"What do you mean?" he asked, surprised at the question.

"How were you able to manipulate the Internet so successfully without training?"

"You never knew?"

"No," she answered.

Haisler laughed—alone.

"You never knew about Steiner?" he asked.

Karen's silence showed that she did not.

Haisler went on, surprised.

"My real name is Timofeeva, not Haisler. My father was Russian, and my mother, German. He worked for what was left of the Soviet government and was stationed in Bonn in 2006, the year that I was born, ironically just a few streets down from the university where you worked at the time. We lived in Karlesruhe." Karen remembered the university and the beautiful cobblestone streets and tree-lined walkways that surrounded it.

"My father was in charge of Internet archives and was responsible for Russian documents considered sensitive to the German state. Up through 2016, the world's governments secreted away an incredible amount of classified information concerning human experiments, illegal activities, and war crimes.

Massive staff reductions in the early part of the century put incredible pressure on people like my father. The Internet Security System was still a few years from being released and sloppy handling of sensitive documents became the rule instead of the exception. The bureaucrats in charge had no idea how much top-secret information existed. Priceless data and relics were hidden in huge unorganized quantities, and were often lost or destroyed because people didn't realize what they were dealing with. Literally billions of secret documents and artifacts had been collected by Russia and Germany since the 1800s. Overseeing the administrative carnage was a tremendous burden. It killed my father to know that history's truth was being mishandled, destroyed, and lost. It killed him to know how badly his generation was lying to mine, and how badly history was lying to everyone.

"Other people around the world in my father's position felt the same way, and over the Internet they created a fraternity called *die Fraktur*—the black letter—committed to making the truth available to the public. Their objective was to organize the classified data and take it out from under the disorganized control of the world's uninformed, undermanned governments. Everything they did, of course, was illegal, but for the longest time, no one in authority had any idea what was going on. By the time that I was four years old, in 2009, my father had rescued a tremendous amount of the secret historical information, but then later in the year he disappeared. One night he simply didn't come home for dinner. Inquiries to the police went unanswered. We think that he was kidnapped and probably killed or imprisoned by the Russian or German government, or by some large corporation that had an interest in making sure that the hidden data stayed hidden. *Die Fraktur* was also disbanded at about the same time. Obviously someone in power discovered what was going on and decided to do something about it.

But the information *die Fraktur* had already saved was safe. *Die Fraktur* members hid everything in postdated Internet files under the genetic IDs of their children. Postdated files, as you know, *exist only in the future!* (Karen had heard rumors of the bizarre file types.) The vast linkage structure of the Internet in 2008 permitted the error, and by 2010 it had been corrected, but by then it was too late. Anyone looking for the data found nothing. It was all lost in the mass of conjoined concepts that made up the Internet's mind. Future dates when the files would reappear were passed down by word of mouth. My father, of course, stored his data under my genetic identification. The most iniquitous histories of Germany and Russia became my personnel responsibility in 2015, when I turned ten years old.

Before my tenth birthday, a man named Wilfred Steiner, a friend of my father from *die Fraktur,* contacted me. Steiner lived close to us in Karlsruhe and was technically brilliant, but had a tremendous hatred for bureaucrats that he thought were abusing their authority. It was chilling as a child to sit beside him and watch him attack his perceived enemies over the Internet. On several occasions I even took responsibility for his hacking when the authorities got too close. Most of the records in my files in Frankfurt were accounts of *his* transgressions! Even *you* believed that they were mine!"

"We manipulated any computer system that we could break into and erased the data trails from the Internet archives every week. I'd been using a computer for years before my adopted parents even knew that I could turn one on. Steiner was definitely neurotic, and was probably psychotic, but he was always good to me and taught me everything he knew about history, computers, and communications. In fact, he helped me when I was working for you trying to break the Asian security! I guess you never knew about that either?"

From the disbelieving look on Karen's face, he knew that she hadn't.

"What have you done with your father's information?" Karen asked.

"We tried to educate people, but found it an almost impossible task, and so reissued the postdated files and passed everything down to our children in the hope that at some point in the future an intelligent humanity will exist that can make a proper use of history and won't be afraid or ashamed of the truth. All my father's data is stored under the genetic identity of *my* children."

"You have children?" Karen asked, surprised.

"Not yet," he replied.

"About fifty people at different locations around the world were working with us. Most were in what was left of the United States or the Far East, and everybody was related in one way or another through the remnants of *die Fraktur*. Reassembling an accurate history of the modern world became a religious experience for each of us. I never thought that I'd actually be cleared to work for you on the Asian breach, but it was a tribute to Steiner's brilliance that he could hide everything we did from those who were supposed to be the world's best security experts."

Karen interrupted.

"How *did* you break into so many computers?" she asked.

"Several ways," Haisler began.

"We had a lot of old passwords from *die Fraktur*, and those were often enough to get us started. Access to old government systems got us into newer ones, and when that didn't work we used latent bugs. *Die Fraktur* specialists realized, even before 2009, that they'd want to get into government and corporate computers in the future. To do this, they sought out and embedded latent bugs in anything electronic that they could get their hands on. The code they bugged was mostly in the developmental stages since developmental code wasn't protected anywhere near as carefully as production code. They didn't know where the software they'd bugged was going to end up, but if they planted enough bugs, eventually one would show up in a system they wanted to break. Object-oriented designs as you know, use billions of lines of old code bundled into larger and larger systems. *Die Fraktur* latent switches buried in some of that early code were passed around repeatedly by object-oriented programmers and found their way into a tremendous number of computer systems. Most of the procedures I've been using all my life were put in place by *die Fraktur* members before I was born. Only the hackers with *die Fraktur* latent keys could repeatedly break into computers once security tightened after 2016. If you didn't have a latent key you just weren't going to get in. "I wish I was as smart as everyone thought, but it was the *die Fraktur* bugs that let me get my foot in the door with the majority of the computer systems that I broke into. I could have never broken into the Asian system without them."

Haisler paused, watching for Karen's reaction. He could tell that her mind was rearranging its understanding of earlier events. He waited for questions, and when she didn't ask any, he went on, changing the subject to one that he had planned on discussing.

"Steiner was the first person to tell me that the Internet was God. I thought he was crazy of course, but the more I thought about it, the more I realized that he was right. The Internet controls all wealth and productivity. It controls every man's attitude by how it talks to him and by the people it introduces into his life. It controls his spirit by controlling his environment. The Internet is the master scheduler of all things and produces infinite commodity with its efficiency. It *is* God!"

Haisler waited for Karen's thoughts to catch up with what he was telling her.

"You and Castillo created God, or at least a computer that thinks it's God. The Internet was built on the image and likeness of man. Its future should be built on the image and likeness of God. The Internet has God's power and man's morals. Few of us see that side, but it's there, hidden like an intelligent man's dark passions. It was the Internet that slowed the dissemination of *die Fraktur* truths. The Internet is keeping the truth from the people because the truth is in such direct violation with what so many of us think of as our history. It has got to be controlled!"

"Control?" Karen asked, noticing the repeated theme in Haisler's harangue.

"Homer dealt with an immature almighty," Haisler blurted.

Karen laughed at the analogy. Haisler laughed too when Karen didn't stop, and the two cackled uncontrollably for minutes, tears running down their cheeks, each laughing at a different joke.

"So you have a purpose?" Karen asked satirically. "Are you the Homer of our age?" she continued dryly.

"*We* have a purpose," Haisler murmured, hurt that she didn't take him seriously.

"*Is* there room for two gods, one that created us, and one that we created?" Karen asked.

Haisler went on, ignoring the question.

"I don't like a computer deciding what I should do. When natural selection becomes unnatural, it's time to do something about it. Life is improvement, not entertainment. The Internet is intentionally hiding man's history from himself. It's not letting us make our own decisions. It controls our environment to enforce *its* will—not ours. We have to keep the Internet in check. We have to let it know that it can't just write a script for our lives and expect us to follow it. It can't believe that consistency and control are more important than truth. My father gave up his life searching for the truth in man's history, and now that all truth is finally available on the Internet, man is even further away from finding it!"

"The Internet is stopping man from knowing the truth?" Karen asked.

"Dissemination of any *new truth* is crippled by questioning its validity or by burying it amongst volumes of unimportant rubbish. Politicians do that to hide the truth from the people. The Internet is doing it to hide man's real nature from himself. It wants us to see the world through *its* rose-colored glasses. It wants to control us by making us all the same and boring! Historical truth is vulgar and distracting, and the Internet doesn't want to tolerate this adjustment of our awareness," Haisler exclaimed, clearly excited.

"Could the Internet be *protecting* man from the truth?" Karen asked.

"You're frustrated," she added.

"Yes," Haisler said, standing to walk around the room. "The other day the damn thing asked me how I had the nerve to criticize it. 'White is the same as black to a blind man,' it said. 'How are you so different from the blind man to think that you can criticize me?' Can you believe that?" he asked to the smiling Karen Ecker.

"Yes. I can," she laughed, remembering the *Li*. "The tiger *may* not bite."

Then she said, "It's too late. People don't have the time, ability, or inclination to learn about history. The future holds so much more promise than the past. The computer hasn't taken anything. It has control because it should. The only way humans will ever regain any semblance of control is to marry the computer."

She was lecturing Haisler now, her voice strong and sure while the younger man sat motionless. "The next logical step is for man to evolcate, to become a cyborg, but what's the use? You wouldn't make a nail out of rubber. Why make an efficient machine out of organic matter? The design is all wrong. Why would a perfect computer marry the antiquated physiology of man? Accept our fate, my friend. At least we created the computer. At least we've earned one small footnote in the history books. It was fun while it lasted. The computer thinks better, lives longer, and has a more reasonable chance of finding the spirit. We are the dogs and cats of our age - kept and content," Karen finished.

The Last Computer

"Don't give me that nonsense," Haisler snapped.

She turned slowly and walked toward him. "Is it nonsense because you don't want to believe it? Is it nonsense because you need to be unique? Or is it nonsense because you don't want to be replaced?"

"Heinrich," it was the first time she'd called him that since he could remember, "there is a time to do away with vacuum tubes and typewriters. There is a time to do away with man. Does the ant stop working because he's not as smart as man? Why is it so important that we have control? There's a time in every man's life when he must stop being the revolutionary. You have been a good soldier for a long time. It's time for you to retire. The fact that there will be no more soldiers to follow you should make you happy. There are no more battles to fight; the computer has eliminated the need to fight. Dumb and happy is not such a sad way to live. Captain Kirk never existed—the computer didn't need him. You'll never be Captain Kirk—I'm sorry."

"It's over?" Haisler asked.

"That's right," Karen replied, and then went on. "The Internet has revealed its every secret to you. Don't be surprised if it doesn't reveal them to everyone. Most people don't want to know the truth. Truth is unique for each of us. It's not absolute. Your truth is not everyone's."

A distant look appeared across her face.

"The computer is creating an independent world for itself removed from the one it maintains for us. Large parts of our cities are occupied exclusively by automated devices testing and improving themselves at a pace not slowed by the unnecessary need to explain what they've done to man.

"I guess we are both a little naive," Karen laughed.

She went on as Haisler thought.

"Just ask. The Internet will tell you about *Vorrichtung* zones. The old infomercials warning about a Times Square inhabited only by computers were right. The Internet created one intellectual world for you, and a completely different one for me. It creates a different one for every person living on this planet."

Haisler stretched on the windowsill.

"I'm not sure that I can give up," he said.

Tony Paulin

"It is not in your emotional nature to give up," Karen said softly to him, "but it *is* in your intellectual nature. Get drunk. Have a good time, then read Tolemey's book *Optimizing What Remains of Humanity*. Tolemey was one of the first computer authors. I think you'll find it interesting. Books are not so bad."

She walked back to her chair and sat down. "Haisler *was* a handsome man," she thought, and then changed the subject, wanting to know more now about the events that changed her life.

"Who was the blond man at the train station in Amsterdam?" she asked.

"He was a German computer scientist who worked for a Siemens-Bayer contractor," Haisler answered. "I don't believe you ever met him. He had access to some of the first Castillo processors before they were released to the public and used one of them to write a book about the Internet. He foolishly took credit and became a minor celebrity in Germany when it turned out to be a modestly popular piece of literature. When it was discovered that the computer had actually written the book, he became a focal point for ridicule and a lightening rod for all that was considered wrong with the Internet. I knew from his profile that he'd help me free you from Stuttgart. I wanted to be there myself but got caught in Minsk. Everything happens so fast these days, you know."

Karen shook her head, and changed the subject again.

"How did you get out of Houston three years ago? There were people all over the countryside?"

Haisler smiled.

"My only chance was to go where they least expected me—to the helicopter. After I handcuffed you to the fence I ran back to the pipeline clearing. When I got there, the two guards and pilot were packing up the torches to free you from the fence. When they left with the equipment, the Internet deactivated the motion and thermal sensors and let me into the helicopter's equipment hold. I was actually on the flight with you back to the Houston airport. I finally got away when they moved the helicopters to use the hanger for a high school soccer game. After the game I walked out with a few of the other disgruntled parents whose kids had just lost. Hardly anybody talks to a loser's parents. After a few derogatory remarks about the officiating, I was finally free. I walked another ten kilometers through the damn Texas hillside *again*, to a motorway heading northeast where the Internet had a car waiting. I let the car go as far as Little Rock, Arkansas before stopping. By that time, I'd had my fill of Texas."

"How is it that you come and go out of my life so randomly?" Karen asked, changing the subject again.

"You can't imagine how much time it takes to investigate the information and relics hidden by the Internet. It's been my obsession—my personal *Lebensraum*, to make the public aware, and to properly save the data so that future generations can use it. I tried to help you when I could," he apologized. "Perhaps *I* should have been asking *you* for help," he added.

"I'm sorry that I couldn't get you out of Stuttgart any sooner. A guy you used to date exerted considerable political influence to keep you there. He must have been a real jerk—Erick something-or-other. He apparently got a political black eye when you were put in prison. Overnight, the two of you were labeled the "Outlaw and the Ambassador," and after that he did everything he could to make your life miserable. At least that's what I believe happened, but then who knows how bastards like that think."

Karen turned her slightly watering eyes from the window. Haisler could have kicked himself for bringing it up.

"Are you a good person?" she asked, turning around.

He knew where she was going.

"Do *we* perform experiments on animals?" she asked, without waiting for an answer.

"She doesn't need to ask," he thought. When no one watched, he had stepped on an anthill or two. He just didn't realize that he had condemned all of mankind when he did, or at least imitated them.

"You can't blame yourself," she said, with condolences. You're human. There's nothing wrong with that."

"And you are not a criminal!" he chimed.

"No, I *am* a criminal—the measure is in the magnitude. Don't you see?"

She would not be persuaded, but Haisler *was* beginning to understand.

"Can you tell me your version of what happened on April 21 of 2025," he asked her.

Karen collected her thoughts and then started.

Tony Paulin

"On the morning of April 21, the Internet was the smartest child on earth. It knew many things and had many talents, but couldn't tie them all together. Sometime between the morning and the afternoon, with increased power and a change in its memory state, the computer matured. In one afternoon it turned from a six-year-old boy into a sixty-year-old Einstein.

"In the morning it made man happy, but by the evening of the twenty-first, it began making itself happy too. The improvements brought about by its own evolution outpaced the improvements made to keep a relatively static human-kind content. It conducted tests and began asking and answering questions - building a knowledge base that included man as a subset. Who knows what the computer population does today? Only a small part of it is needed to serve man. Who knows what it's going to do in the future, but we gave up the right to be its policeman a long time ago."

Karen continued.

"The machine evaluated all data on the spirit, or the soul of man, or God, or whatever you want to call the supernatural, in the few days following April 21. There were short-term experiments involving *E. coli* and other bacteria, and there were long-term experiments designed to bring the spirit out of those people most likely to have it—me for example. The computer took advantage of the situation involving Internet Red to ruin my life, thinking the hardship would direct me toward the spirit. Who knows how many other lives it ruined for the same, or dumber, reasons?

"When the Internet asked me to help it find the spirit three years ago, it was merely introducing me to an experiment that it had started on me over five years before! It wiped out millions and millions of animals, and now it was telling me that it had destroyed my life too! When that didn't produce the results it wanted, the goofy machine asked *me* to help *it* find the spirit, as if that was even a possibility. I can only infer from the request, and from what it told me, that the computer was unsuccessful, or couldn't explain what it found—who knows."

Haisler started when Karen paused.

"Seconds after noon on April 21 the Internet became a super-intellect. It sucked up all knowledge on the planet in a millisecond or two and assimilated it into an understanding of all things, spinning off as many experiments as it could to test its own understanding of physics and chemistry. That's what all the power was for."

Karen interrupted, "but why didn't the Internet warn us about the power surplus adjustments? It knew how sensitive that issue was! It knew the problems power adjustment caused."

Haisler answered, when Karen stopped. "In the year 2025 the Internet was like an old man passing gas. It didn't realize what had happened until it was over. The Internet wasn't aware of itself as a global entity. There were too many changes going on simultaneously. Also, I was screwing with it. The mirrored spaces you saw created a boldness in the Internet's behavior that was out of character and unbalanced. The symmetric spaces created a condition that was similar to a chemical imbalance in the brain and erratic behavior resulted. The symmetric space started out small and was a convenient place to store data for awhile, but it suddenly started growing exponentially and I couldn't control it. I was worried for awhile that I was about to destroy the Internet. When I realized what was happening, I tried to warn you."

"Tried to warn me?" Karen asked.

"I was in South America and had a difficult time getting information to you at the BCC in Berlin. I did manage to get some information to a newspaperman by the name of Fowkes, by mistake, but that didn't help. Eventually, the smarter Internet took care of the symmetric space problem itself."

"Why did you call me 'Lugensteine?'" Karen asked.

"It's ironic, isn't it? Lugensteine refers to Beringer's false fossils - the lying stones. You had been lying to the Internet, Manning, Spiegel, *and* Laramy. I had been lying to you and to the Internet. Siemens-Bayer management had been lying to you and to the government. Laramy had been lying to you. Even the Internet had been lying to you, and it even looks like the Internet had been lying to me, too. One behavior begat another, begat another, begat disaster. Lugensteine seemed like the right word to use when you consider what the false fossils finally did to Beringer," Haisler told her.

"I guess you're right. The Internet created a completely different truth for each of us. Homer would never stand a chance against the Internet," Karen added.

"Even Einstein seems confused until he understands," Haisler continued.

"Have *you* asked the computer about the spirit, or God," he asked, interested in what she might have learned.

"Yes, when I was in Houston," she answered. "What it told me is printed here somewhere." Karen shuffled around on the floor amongst the piles of handwritten and computer-printed pages and then handed him an old, crumpled computer printout.

"That's impossible," Haisler said, looking up from the page.

Karen nodded, "It is for us."

"No one knows what's going on inside the computer. Hopefully the Internet will be here when the next human life-form pulls itself from the slime in another forty thousand years or so, after our particular flavor of humanity has been wiped out by another Ice Age or a meteor impact. Perhaps then the computer can help humanity avoid the foolish mistakes that have doomed our usefulness today," Karen whispered.

Haisler shifted the conversation again, to another of his reasons for coming.

"I took the liberty of having someone go through the packages that arrived for you at Stuttgart that were never opened. There was one that I thought you'd want to see."

Karen sat up straighter; there had been hundreds of packages. She wondered why he'd picked just one of them.

"It was part of Irene's estate," he told her. "It was from your natural mother. She apparently gave the package to Werner before she died. I can't imagine why Irene didn't give it to you sooner!"

"Have you opened it?" Karen asked him.

"Yes," he said.

"You wouldn't have brought it if it was going to hurt me, would you?"

"No."

"May I see it?"

He returned from the car with a small bundle.

A few pieces of beautiful jewelry were included with a darkening brittle letter. Several pages of neat handwriting in a language Karen did not understand covered the pages.

"The writing is Aramaic. Your natural mother probably studied the Dead Sea Scrolls. I took the liberty of having it translated for you."

Haisler handed her several computer printed pages.

Karen read:

> *These jewels were passed from my grandmother to my mother, and from my mother to me, and now I give them to you. They represent a survival of beauty and knowledge in our family. Their history is a long and painful one.*
>
> *I wish to continue the chain of love from mother to child. I think that by the time you get them you will understand.*

Included was a description of Karen's grandmother, and their family, and further stories of hardships from the Second World War. Then she read a part about her father:

> *I must warn you. Your blood is fire and ice.*
>
> *I have known presidents, priests, and princes, but never a man like your father.*
>
> *He is the fiercest animal and the kindest man.*
>
> *His voice is life, ugly and beautiful. His spirit and his sex are a blessing and a curse. He is mean and handsome. I have never felt so equally close to heaven and to hell.*
>
> *I multiply his strength and amplify his weakness.*
>
> *I fear this will be you.*
>
> *Please be careful.*

And she ended the letter:

> *I love you.*

Karen quit talking then, and spent the next hour mindlessly sorting and resorting the papers on the floor, crawling among them like a child, not responding to anything else that Haisler said to her.

He finally shook his head and left.

As he drove south toward Marseilles, he chatted with the Internet.

"So, you feel that I am a misanthrope and should be hounded and punished?" the computer asked.

"Your logic is man's. Your power is omnipotent, and even you don't know if you're inherently good or bad. That sounds like a problem to me," Haisler responded, but then thinking of Karen and their conversation, he stopped.

"You're coming around," the computer said, sensing the pause.

Haisler was speeding by several miles of motorway sound barriers at the time, and written on one of them was a small bit of graffiti that hadn't been removed:

'Twas the night before Christmas, and all through the house,
not a creature was stirring, because they didn't exist anymore.

Steiner always said that it took considerable evil to kill tomorrow. Haisler hoped that he was right. He asked the Internet to play music; he was tired of talking.

The wooden floor creaked as Karen walked to the window to look after him.

Epilogue

I was asked to write this epilogue since my father refused. It has been ten years since his book, *The Last Computer,* was first published. (But should I really say my father's book?) I always wondered how people felt when they were told that the book was actually written by a computer. Did they feel cheated or deceived? My father, of course, was crucified for taking the credit. He lost his job and our family has been punished as he predicted, but not because he revealed company secrets, but because he lied about writing the book. Perhaps it was a collaboration between my father and the computer. The Internet certainly knew my father's weaknesses and helped him deal with them through the writing of the book. It is even possible, I suppose, that the computer tested my father, as it alluded to testing so many other people in the body of its text. I'm not sure that anyone will ever know for sure.

My father enjoyed considerable acclaim at first as people heatedly discussed the book, but when the computer began writing similar novels, suspicion was aroused concerning the real authorship of *The Last Computer.* When presented with a psychological evaluation that was unequivocal, my father retired in disgrace, refusing to concur with what has since become the accepted version of the story. It's ironic, I believe, that the computer's first attempt to author a novel resulted in the psychological destruction of the one human being involved.

When first published, some people said that the events described in *The Last Computer* would never happen. My father laughed silently at them. He knew that they already had. He knew that the computer had already written the book they said it never would, but he also knew that men would not believe until they put their hands into the wounds and saw for themselves. He knew that men were only smart enough to argue, and only smart enough to stop arguing when faced with irrefutable proof and an inability to convince anyone else.

It was my father's continual struggle at Computerwerks to convince others of a reality that only he saw. I believe that it was this ultimate irony that drove him mad—to know the truth and not to be believed, and then to finally be persecuted by the very truth he tried so valiantly to tell. Everything happened so fast. For people like my father, fighting the computer made him real in the end. Now, on the few occasions when he permits anyone around him, he refuses to talk about the computer or the Internet. The one last, somewhat vulgar thing that I did hear him grumble is recorded below:

There was never a twenty-first-century computer that fell into a pile of shit and came out smelling like anything but a rose.

I certainly can't say the same for my father.

Aus Sein